# BETTER

# SCRAMBLE

# THAN

# LOSE

# BETTER

# SCRAMBLE

# THAN

# LOSE

Fran Tarkenton
as told to Jack Olsen

**SCHOLASTIC BOOK SERVICES**

NEW YORK • TORONTO • LONDON • AUCKLAND • SYDNEY

A hardcover edition of this book is published by
Four Winds Press, a division of Scholastic, and is
available through your local bookstore or directly
from Four Winds Press, 50 West 44 Street, New
York, New York 10036.

1st printing .................................................. November 1969

Printed in the U. S. A.

# 1

They call me The Scrambler. It's a nickname that is not entirely accurate, but if George Herman Ruth did not mind being called The Babe who am I to object to being called The Scrambler? One thing that bothers me about having the name hung on me is that it's a little misleading. Sure, I scramble. When everything else breaks down, I don't hesitate to roam out of the pocket and do the boogaloo. I don't automatically fall down and go boom when I'm trapped just because that's what quarterbacks traditionally do. These wild sideline-to-sideline scrambles have become my trademark. People have forgotten the simple truth of the matter, which is that I'm basically a pocket passer — just as much a pocket passer as four out of five of the professional quarterbacks in the game.

Through the years, lots of quarterbacks have been called scramblers — the name was hung on Frank Ryan when he played at Los Angeles a decade ago, but it didn't stick — and a few writers applied it to me in my first couple of years. But it wasn't until we played in New York in 1964, when I was with the Minnesota Vikings, that the name was tattooed on me for good. We beat the Giants, and next day all you could read in the New York papers was stuff about The Scrambler and Scrambling Fran. There wasn't a reporter who covered the game who didn't tell his readers about the time "the eel-like Minnesota quarterback" popped out of the pocket, roamed 40 yards behind the line of scrimmage, and finally completed a pass downfield for a 10-yard gain. Several writers called me The Scrambler, and the name was mine forever. And how many times do you think I scrambled in that ball game? Once.

That's right. All those thousands of words and tons of newsprint and gallons of printer's ink were based on one out of 29 times I handled the ball. There were other times during that game when I ran the ball — doesn't every quarterback? — but you couldn't have called those plays scrambles in the remotest sense of the word.

It makes a fellow wonder just what a scrambler is, and sometimes I'm tempted to offer the following definition: "A scrambler is somebody the press calls a scrambler." But that wouldn't be quite fair, either. I *do* scramble. I *do* get on some pretty hairy journeys out there. But how often? I once sat down and studied my style over a period of six or seven games, and here is what I came up with: On the average I would call 28 pass plays a game. On 25 of them I would stay in the planned pattern; on three of them I would scramble. If that doesn't make me a pocket passer, then figures are meaningless. As for scrambling efficiency, I completed a pass on half of my scrambles, one fourth of the time I made yardage running, and one fourth of the time I got dumped.

After the tag The Scrambler had become mine, all mine, the public misconceptions about me seemed to multiply. I'd play a game away from home and I'd scramble maybe two or three times, which was my average, and after the game all the reporters would come to me and ask, "Why didn't you play your usual style?" And "How come you threw so much from the pocket?" And I would try to say, "I threw from the pocket because that is my style."

"No, it isn't," they would say. "You're a scrambler."

"Okay," I would say. "I'm a scrambler." Anything to get to the shower.

The public attitude about scrambling is a conglomeration of a lot of wrong ideas, and I'm not trying to put a rap on the public, because there are plenty of men intimately involved in pro football who are just as confused about what a scrambler is. You'd be surprised how much the pro football people believe what they read. Things get printed over and over again, many of them wrong, and once a fundamental mistake has been printed, you can never catch up with it and straighten it out. For example, somebody once printed that the basic motivation for my scrambling was fear. And since then I've read that theory at least a hundred times. But *it was said as a joke!* Exactly the same thing happened years ago when Norm Van Brocklin said, "I only run from stark fear!"

This is part of the modesty of any quarterback when he's being interviewed. You turn questions aside with jokes, because otherwise you're going to have to say things like, "Sure, I scramble because I'm good at it, because I can twist and dodge those big pass rushers better than most guys and we get a lot of touchdowns that way." If *that* comes out in the papers, everybody says, "Boy, that Tarkenton has a big head, doesn't he?" So you shrug your shoulders and you tell the reporters with a fetching smile, "Aw, I only run from fear," and everybody laughs, and then the same line pops up in the newspapers and the readers take it seriously. Why, the idea that any pro football player would run from fear is ridiculous on the face of it. A quarterback has to maintain his cool while a 300-pound pass rusher is firing at him like a Sidewinder missile and, at the last second before his feet get knocked out from under him, he has to stick that ball right on some receiver's left ear. To perform in that sort of pattern over and over again, you've got to be entirely lacking in fear or sense, one or the other, and if you lacked sense you wouldn't be playing the pro game anyway.

I don't know anything in pro football that has been as overemphasized and as misconstrued as my occasional scrambling. Even the NFL helps spread the misconception. Every year the league gets up a film called *NFL Highlights,* and every year I'll run maybe two really *wild* scrambles during the whole season, and guess what you'll see me doing in *NFL Highlights*? It's been that way for years. I don't blame the guys who make the NFL films; scrambles are exciting and unusual and sometimes even funny. A few years ago, as usual, I was in the NFL film for two plays — both scrambles. One of them is against Dallas. It's third and four on our own 45-yard line and I fake a handoff to the halfback going to the right and now I'm supposed to throw to my right end, who has faked a block and sneaked to the opposite side of the field. The only trouble is, some Dallas defenders have sneaked right with him, and the pass rush is boring in on me, so I take off. I run to the right and nothing develops downfield, so I wheel off to the left, about 10 yards behind the line, and there's still nobody home. I wheel back

9

to the right again, and then back to the left again, and all this takes about 35 seconds, and pass receivers and the defensive secondary are whirling around downfield like bugs on a millpond. Finally, somebody breaks into the clear and I hit him for a 10-yard gain and a first down.

The other scramble was against San Francisco, late in the game, and I can't find a receiver open, so I break out of the pocket and run around to my left, and pretty soon the 49er pass rushers have me cornered. I wheel back to the middle of the field and stop to throw, but there's still nobody open and a guy is flying at me, so I take off again and the guy sails right over me, and then I run all the way over to the sideline and throw a long pass to the goal line. One of the defenders tips it up in the air and my man catches it for a touchdown. How are you going to leave plays like that off the NFL highlight film? And millions of viewers see the film and they say, "Boy, those Minnesota Vikings sure come up with some interesting game plans." They don't understand that the scramble is never planned, it is a reaction to an emergency. It just happens, and a lot less often than people have been led to believe.

But if you never understood scrambling before, don't feel bad. Neither do a lot of people who ought to know better. Three days before the Pro Bowl Game one year, Coach Don Shula of the Baltimore Colts came up to me and said, "Fran, anytime you're ready we'll be glad to work on your scrambles for a while." He actually thought we had scramble plays that could be practiced. Later that day, Don McCafferty, one of Shula's assistants, took me aside and said, "Fran, tell me something. Do you scramble off the rollout, off the bootleg, or when?"

I said, "Coach, you scramble off the busted play, that's all. You do it when you can't do anything else."

Another time, Colt tackle Bob Vogel asked Viking tackle Grady Alderman, "Grady, what kind of blocking patterns do you have for The Scrambler?" Grady said, "Well, we don't really have any patterns. All you do is just stand still and wait for old Fran to come past you again. And if you miss your man the first time, don't worry. Fran'll be back." Grady was kidding, of course, that's one of his favorite lines. The truth is, you block for the scramble the same way you block for any other play. You knock down everybody in your assigned area and after that you knock down everybody in sight. There's no special pattern. And, anyway, when I'm scrambling it's because something has broken down — me, the pass blocking, or the pattern. That's why I'm scrambling.

I don't mean to grumble about being called The Scrambler — in a way, I have become rather fond of the nickname — but I would like to make it evident that the whole thing has been played way out of proportion. It has become a psychological thing in some cases. Defensive linemen who are going to be playing against me sometimes get unduly worried about my scrambling. They tell themselves, "Oh, me, I can't let him get to the outside. And I can't let him get inside." They get all worked up about it and they have special drills where they practice chasing a quarterback all over the field so that they'll be ready for me. That's fine with me. I'm glad they're spending their time on defending against my scrambles because I know I never scramble that much and that leaves them less time to prepare for other things.

There is no better example of what I'm talking about than what happened one time when I was with the Vikings. In that game we upset the Packers because they were so preoccupied with my scrambling. Their defense tried to play a game of containing me, of not letting me get to the outside. They decided not to put on their usual forceful rush, choosing instead to keep me in the pocket and that way keep me from scrambling. We ate them up that day. After the game the Packers admitted that they had made a mistake. It's the same mistake that so many others have made, for they've convinced themselves that I spend the whole day scrambling. That afternoon they learned that I scramble only when necessary.

Another misconception is that the mobile,

scrambling quarterback is a marked man. As John Unitas once said, "I have to believe that a rollout quarterback cannot last very long, because he does such a lot of running around with big guys hitting him in the open. You can only take so much of that. Then again, his receivers are not likely to last too long either, because they have to keep scrambling like passers until the opportunity for a catch occurs." Don Shula seemed to feel the same way. Several years ago he said, "The running quarterback is not for Baltimore. We have only two, John Unitas and Gary Cuozzo, and want to keep them both healthy."

Well, the very year that Don made that statement he lost both his quarterbacks to injuries and had to play Tom Matte, a halfback. It turned out that staying in the pocket was no guarantee of safety at all. When I first went to the Vikings, everybody would see me scramble and they'd say, "He'll get killed doing that." But in my first years at Minnesota it didn't make any difference if I was killed or not. No championship was hanging on me; we weren't going to win many games as a new franchise team anyway, and we were all expendable. So I scrambled all over the field. Sure, I took some lumps, but in six years at Minnesota I missed maybe a total of two quarters in 84 games.

Some people say it's all well and good to scramble at my age, which is 29, but as soon as I get a little older and lose a step or two, they'd better start selecting my tombstone. I don't agree at all. Scrambling isn't a matter of speed, it's a matter of quickness, and I believe a man can maintain his essential quickness till he's 40 or even beyond. I think a player can even *increase* his quickness, if he doesn't let himself get out of shape in the off-season and if he works at it all the time. I watched Gino Marchetti play when he was 39 and he was as quick and effective as he was when he was 29. Maybe in the 100-yard dash he was a second slower, but that has nothing to do with anything. I expect to be playing when I'm 39, and I expect to be scrambling my usual two or three plays a game, and I hope to be in the flower of health.

One reason I have been injured so seldom is that I move around a lot. Quarterbacks who are hit while standing still are jolted by the full force of the tackle and are often badly shaken or hurt. I can't say that I haven't been shaken up a number of times, but by floating and scrambling I present a moving target and when I do get floored I'm better able to absorb the shock.

Now we're getting into an area that I think has caused much misunderstanding and which led to my being called The Scrambler — namely, the distinction between floating and scrambling. When a quarterback drops back into the pocket to pass, he often must jockey for position so that he can find a receiver. The quarterback's field of vision is the single most important aspect of passing. Unless a passer can locate his receiver and can see what the secondary is up to, he is out of business. It is the job of the front four — the defensive ends and tackles — to block this field of vision. Today's front four are bigger, stronger, and, somehow, more mobile than ever. They come stomping in on the quarterback with thunderous force and with arms outstretched. Trying to escape their clutches is one considerable task. Another is trying to establish a field of vision, to remain calm and get a reading on what is going on downfield. To be able to do this requires movement or floating by the quarterback. Because I have been labeled The Scrambler, many people tend to feel that this floating around I do is scrambling.

All quarterbacks float to some extent. Coach Hank Stram of Kansas City has come up with what he calls the "floating pocket" for his quarterback, Lenny Dawson. Quarterbacks today move more than they ever have and this is primarily because they have to move in order to elude those hard-charging defensive linemen. This idea of moving around is not really so different now, except that when I came into the league in 1961, Norm Van Brocklin was *the* quarterback of the time, the prototype of his era. He was also my coach on the Vikings. Those were the days when coaches were sticklers for quarterbacks dropping back seven yards and not moving. Much was written about how Van Brocklin never ran with the ball. Well, the reason he didn't run was because he couldn't run. His arm was worth its weight in gold, but his legs were like lead. For him to have run would have been foolish.

Modern quarterbacks are movers. Even Joe Namath of the Jets floats around. Very seldom does he drop back, set up, and pass. He floats at between 10 and 12 yards, he establishes his field of vision, and then he lets go. A lot of people talk about Joe's lack of mobility because of his bad legs. Actually, if his legs were all that bad he wouldn't have the mobility to get back 10 or 12 yards. Some folks think that Namath drops back so far in order to protect his knees, to keep himself out of the range of those defensive linemen. Not so. His real reason is so that he can get a clear view of the skirmishes downfield as his receivers try to break into the open.

I've talked to quite a few defensive linemen and they've told me, "If we know that the quarterback is going to be in the same position all the time, it makes our job much easier. If he's just going to drop straight back seven yards and set up, then we can zero in on the same spot all day." But if the defensive lineman has to worry about whether the quarterback is going to throw from seven yards one time and from 12 yards the next, and about whether he's going to throw from behind right tackle on one play and from behind left tackle on the next, then he's in a quandary. Floating around doesn't solve a quarterback's problems, though. Defensive linemen are not that easily outwitted. Now they counter with a sophisticated rush. No longer can the passer be certain that those front four are going to come at him from the same routes. They twist between the tackle and the end, and they have inside moves and outside moves, and you can never count on what lane they're going to use to get to you. This is why quarterbacks everywhere are floating. Forget about the notion that we're trying to protect ourselves by floating around. This is just not so. Our primary job is not to protect ourselves. We're out there to win games and we have to complete passes in order to do so. To accomplish this we must roam or float so that we can find our receivers.

Right now you're witnessing a time of marked change in professional football, a time in which we're moving toward a more wide-open, imaginative, fluid offense. The aim is to get the ball into the end zone in any way possible, and that includes rolling it if necessary. I'm all for this approach. I'll do whatever it takes to get across that goal line, whether it's running, passing, or scrambling, kicking or crawling, or lateralling, or standing on my head, I'm willing to do it, and I expect everybody else on the New York Giants to feel the same way.

The most exciting thing happening to offensive football right now is the increasing number of formations that are being exploited. Dallas Coach Tom Landry was the first to use this brand of offensive football. Baltimore has been doing the same thing lately. Before long, I think that all teams will have more variety in their offense.

For many years, offensive football was basically built around two formations. One was called the Brown Formation — that's what most pro teams called it — and it had the fullback stationed behind the quarterback, and the halfbacks on either side. The other formation is what we have called the Open, or Red, Formation. In this setup the fullback was placed behind one tackle, and one of the halfbacks behind the other tackle. Each formation had its strengths — and weaknesses. The Brown is the one that Jimmy Brown of Cleveland and Jim Taylor of Green Bay made famous. They would run the slant to the weak side, where they would have a halfback blocking for them. But the Brown Formation was not good for running wide to the strong side. The Red Formation called for trapping the defensive end and it was from this alignment that the Green Bay sweep-plays were used. This formation was not nearly as effective on plays to the other side, for the tight end was not available to trap the defensive end and open a path.

Oh, there were variations of these formations

but the game of chess between offense and defense was becoming rather simplified. The defense was able to key to these formations and the offense was simply not coming up with new ways to confound the defenders. Then they started going to the double wing, taking the halfback and putting him a yard behind the line as a receiver. That gave you four receivers at or near the line of scrimmage. Next came the triple-flanker formation in which the tight end, the halfback, and the flanker were all used. Then they started to flop receivers, taking the tight end and the weak side end and switching positions. What they were trying to do was to get the two fastest pass receivers on the same side. That gave the defense plenty to think about. Was the defense going to be willing, or able, to switch a cornerback all the way over to a safety position in order to get its speed men on the two fastest receivers? Forcing the defense to prepare for these variations created more room for error. It used to be that it was the defense that confused the offense with its blitzes and its diverse forms of coverage, but now it is the offense that is forcing the defense to adjust and think. The more time that defensive players have to spend adjusting and thinking, the less time they have to react. Football is a game of freeing the mind of as much clutter as possible so that you can concentrate on playing. Now it is the offense that is jamming the defense, giving it more to think about than ever. This wide-open kind of game is going to produce the most exciting football ever seen.

Green Bay dominated the game for most of the 1960's. There is always a tendency to mimic a successful style, but despite this most National Football League teams use a very different style. The Packers raised their theory to the highest level, emphasizing execution, sophistication, and discipline, and there's nothing wrong with that. But there's also a place for imagination and verve and flair for improvisation, for trying everything, for breaking out of there and turning a busted play into a long gain.

Furthermore, I'll go so far as to say that flexibility and mobility have NFL history on their side, and that Green Bay's style goes *against* the pattern of football history. The whole trend has been from the static to the mobile, from the planned to the improvised. Remember the days when seven guys used to line up with their shoulder pads almost touching, and seven other guys would line up across from them and when the ball was centered everybody began to shove? Then the defense became more mobile: They would jump from four-three to five-three to five-two, and change assignments and stunt and blitz and do all kinds of crazy things, and pretty soon the offensive lines had to open up and become more flexible themselves. And look at the backfield. The ball used to be centered to one back and he would take off like a truck, following some "blocking back" who would lead him into the line, and together they would try to shove open a hole.

Compare that with the mobility in a backfield nowadays. It's all moving, kaleidoscopic, *fluid*, and to my mind the immobile quarterback no longer has a place in that kind of game. It used to be perfectly normal for a quarterback to duck his head and take an automatic eight-yard loss whenever the pattern didn't develop downfield. Well, my philosophy is that I've got to go for the first down with everything I've got and, if the play looks like it's turning into a disaster, then I believe I should get out of that pocket and try to make something out of the broken play. Let's say I'm on my own 40-yard line and it's third and eight and I go back and the protection breaks down and the pass rush is right on top of me. All right, I can unfurl the white flag and take an eight-yard loss. Or I can move out and risk taking a longer loss and at the same time keep my chances alive for a first down. To me, there's no choice.

Up at Minnesota, we would use any weapon to move the football. We even made wholesale use of the lateral, and there was one year when almost every offensive lineman on our club had at least one carry. We'd start to be tackled and we'd just flip the ball back to the nearest man in a Viking uniform, and we scored a lot of touchdowns that way. People would say, "My, my, how bush." And

21

we would go right on lateralling, maybe eight or 10 times a season on the average, and in my six years at Minnesota we never lost the ball on a lateral.

Once at Los Angeles we won on a double lateral. I was trapped, flipped the ball to Mick Tingelhoff, our center, and he unloaded to Bill Brown, who ran for a touchdown. After that game, David Jones, the Los Angeles defensive end, said, "That play won't work against anybody but us, but you can expect anything from Tarkenton. He might lateral the ball to a fan!" In another game, it was fourth and 10 and we needed to score a touchdown. A field goal would do us no good. When the pass receivers showed up covered, I ran the ball down to the five-yard line and that was the end of the road — I was surrounded by unfriendly faces. Out of the corner of my eye I spotted fullback Bill McWatters about half a mile away and behind me, so I turned and passed him a lateral, and he went in untouched. Dangerous? Sure. But what if he missed it, or what if he fumbled? We'd have lost anyway. So it was sandlot. Who cares? It was our only chance. It didn't bother us if we looked bad winning. That beats looking good losing!

The craziest play we ever ran at Minnesota was against Green Bay, of all teams. The time was 1964, and I hadn't yet learned that the way to beat Green Bay was to play them at their own conservative, careful game. As a result, we were down by a score of 23-21 and there was just a little more than a minute left. We had the ball, first and 10, in our own territory. On the first play, the Green Bay pass rush got to me and I took an eight-yard loss. On the next play we got hit with a five-yard penalty and lost the down. On third down, Tom Michel gained one yard on a running play. Now with fourth down and 22 yards to go, there were 54 seconds left, and Green Bay went into the fiercest looking "prevent" defense you ever saw, with about six dozen defenders stationed all over the field to stop the home run. I called time and announced my plans. "Fellows," I said, "there's nothing on our ready list that'll help us now. We've got to do something drastic, and here's what it is: I want you ends to go down the field 25 yards, turn, and hook up. You backs go straight out. That'll make five guys out there. I'm gonna scramble around till I can find one of you open."

They all looked at me as if I was nuts, and maybe I was. It was the only scramble I'd ever *called*.

I knew I'd never have time to find a receiver on a normal drop, so I took the ball and spun out to the right, and as usual Willie Davis was right on my tail. (It wouldn't have surprised me to see Willie and me voted "cutest couple" after some of those Green Bay-Minnesota games; he was always clawing at me.) Anyway, I had to retreat all the way to my own 10-yard line to get away from Willie. I set up to throw, and I felt his hand on my heel, so I pulled away from him again, and then way down the field I spotted Tom Hall in the clear on the right sideline. I got the pass away, right on a line toward Tom, and then out of the corner of my eye I saw a white shirt streaking toward Hall and into the flight of the ball. It was our tight end, Gordie Smith. He saw that ball in the air and he was going to catch it! I said, "No, Gordie! No! No!" but he kept right on going and he plucked that ball right out of Tom Hall's hands and went down to the Green Bay 27-yard line. We used up a little time and then Fred Cox came in and kicked the field goal that gave us our first win over the Packers.

Of course, if the scramble always worked that well even Green Bay would be using it, and I have to admit that sometimes the results of a scramble are less than spectacular. In a game against Detroit, I kept moving backward, with Alex Karras and Darris McCord all over me, and finally I wound up on my own 10-yard line, 45 yards from the line of scrimmage, and now what do I do? I broke upfield and got back 32 yards. The whole place was in an uproar, and I got a standing ovation when I was finally tackled for a 13-yard loss! One of our linemen threw three blocks on the play. People kept shouting: "Look out! Here he comes again!"

I probably hold the record for the longest fumble in pro football, and this was off a scramble, too. We were playing the Rams in our first or second year and I didn't have very good judgement in those days. The Rams put on a blitz and this is the worst possibile time to scramble, but I rolled out anyway, into all that traffic. I wheeled to my right and nobody was open, and a couple of Ram defenders were all over me, so I wheeled to my left, and nobody was open, and all the time I was dropping further and further behind the line of scrimmage. Finally, one of those big L. A. linemen hit my arm and the ball squirted out. Somebody kicked it even further toward our goal line trying to pick it up, and then Los Angeles fell on the ball. The total loss was 45 yards! That's how I learned that the scramble is not the answer to a blitz.

Down through the years, I've had a lot of fun with those giants who go after me when I scramble. They huff and they puff and they get all red in the face. They're hauling 275 pounds around, and I'm only hauling 190. Sometimes they get downright sore about it. Once, Big Daddy Lipscomb spent the whole afternoon trying to nail me and finally he did, and I flattened out under his 300 pounds like a dead cat on a superhighway.

He's making no effort to get off me, he's sitting there gasping for breath, and finally he says, "Little man, why fo' you run so much?" The great Los Angeles pass rusher, David Jones, says that he has to chase me all over the field so much that when he does catch me, he's too tired to enjoy it. And Alex Karras once said, "He wears you out. I'd like to get my hands on the son of a gun just once, but I can't catch him." How I wish that were true!

I think my shining hour in the personal war department came against Chicago, where Doug Atkins always made me a special project when I scrambled. I spent many an anxious moment under Doug wondering how many of my ribs were left, but on this particular occasion I got away from his grip about three times and finally made a 37-yard gain with Doug chasing me all the way. When the play was over, Doug didn't have the breath to say a word. He just walked off the field and motioned to Coach George Halas to put somebody in till he got his wind.

Scrambles like that stick in people's minds and a lot of times it's been said that my scrambles are leading the way toward a new kind of offensive pro football. That's a little exaggerated. George Svendsen, a scout for the San Francisco 49ers, was quoted as saying, "That jumping-jack, Mr. Tarkenton, will mark the newest trend in the evolution of the game. From now on you'll see more and more scrambling by quarterbacks. They'll roll out more, be more mobile. They've got to do something to get away from that pass rush."

I wish I could accept that kind of statement as gospel truth but, in my opinion, I am following the trend, the trend is not following me. Quarterbacks with the ability to move around have been with us for many years. Some of the finest quarterbacks in recent years have exhibited excellent mobility. Don Meredith of the Dallas Cowboys majors in a rollout offense. Maybe he doesn't scramble all the way back to the five-yard line the way I've done on occasion, but he throws from outside the pocket routinely and he can scramble when he has to. Frank Ryan moved around plenty when he brought two consecutive Eastern championships to Cleveland, and John Brodie was throwing from all over the place when he led his team to the number one spot in total offense at San Francisco. Bart Starr scrambles and big Roman Gabriel, who is 6'3½" and 225 pounds, runs well. Even some of the quarterbacks of bygone years had a lot of maneuverability. Tobin Rote was one of those who ran with the ball and so did Bobby Layne. Y. A. Tittle came up as a single-wing tailback and he knew how to move when the going got tough. Otto Graham roamed all over the backfield and so did Sammy Baugh.

I think that the quarterback of tomorrow will be better than we are today, and he'll be able to do a zillion things, including scrambling. He's going to have the ability to throw from the roll, the moving pocket, the dropback pocket, the bootleg, and the busted play. What you're seeing now is the turnover period. When the present crop of pro quarterbacks goes out (and many of them are already over 30), the new group will make us old-timers look silly. The quarterbacks coming out of colleges nowadays are better athletes than ever before: They can do everything. They're just not producing any more of those stay-in-the-pocket, rocking-chair quarterbacks. The new breed will make the game of football wilder and more interesting than ever before. You'll see a mobile, unstereotyped game, a fluid, intellectual, complex game, sort of like chess with a crunch. You'll see more rollouts, more bootlegs, more scrambles, more moving pockets, more play-pass action, more multiple formations — not only the flanker formation or flanker with split ends, but the double and triple wing, with three flankers to one side, or the wing double wing, or maybe variations of the shotgun. There will be all kinds of offenses and they will *all be used by the same team in the same game.*

One of the joys of playing for the New York Giants is that Coach Allie Sherman has told me that he considers my scrambling an asset, some-

thing to be exploited, not just something to be p
up with. He's willing to work with me and he's
willing to take advantage of every technique in
the book to get points up on the scoreboard. Sherman has imagination and, believe me, it took a
vivid imagination back in 1967 when I joined
the Giants to think that the team would be a
winner. He guided the team through a difficult
period of adjustment and has all of us on the
squad thinking not just of winning but of winning
the championship — and that's what football is
all about.

# 2

I didn't play much at all in the very first game in Minnesota Vikings' history. It was an exhibition game in Sioux Falls, S. D., against the Dallas Cowboys. George Shaw started at quarterback for us, and I sat on the bench, where a green kid from the University of Georgia belonged, although I didn't believe it at the time. I thought the green kid from Georgia was good enough to start for the Minnesota Vikings or any other professional football team, which shows you how much I knew.

By the start of the fourth quarter of that first exhibition game, we hadn't scored a touchdown, and Coach Norm Van Brocklin told me to take over. I ran out there, full of vim and vitality, and bang-bang-bang we scored on a pass. Boy, this was easy! All these years the quarterbacks of the National Football League had been spreading their propaganda about how tough it was in the NFL, and now I knew it wasn't any tougher than a sandlot game on the corner of Broad and Lumpkin Streets in my hometown of Athens, Ga. We lost the game, but I was elated. I was on a peak. I'd always hoped that I'd be able to make it in the pros, and now I knew there would be no problem.

To my amazement, Van Brocklin started George Shaw in the next game, against the Baltimore Colts at Baltimore. I was under the impression that I had arrived the week before, and here I was still being treated like a rookie. Even Stubby Eason, the equipment manager, didn't understand that I was now an established player. Before the game he came up to me and said, "Rookie, you better take that single face bar off your helmet and put on a double like all the rest of the quarterbacks."

"No," I said, "one bar is plenty for me. I wouldn't be able to see out of a double." I'd played four years of college ball at Georgia with a single face bar, and I didn't need an equipment manager changing my whole way of life at this stage of the game.

Our attack didn't do much in the first quarter against Baltimore, and just after the start of the second quarter, Van Brocklin hollered, "Okay, Peach, get in there!" I ran out on the field ready to pick the Colts apart like a chicken. It didn't matter to me that I had collected bubble gum pictures of some of these very same Baltimore defensive players, that they were recognized stars, that the Colts were the big noise in professional football. I was no amateur myself.

I figured I'd show everybody right off that I wasn't afraid to get into the action, so in the huddle I said, "Open four right, screen right to four," which meant a screen pass to Mel Triplett, the tough runner we got in a trade from the New York Giants. I took the snap from center, dropped back into the pocket and set up, faked to one receiver and then lofted the ball out to Triplett in the right flat. The pass looked like perfection itself: I was standing there admiring its trajectory, its spiral, its pinpoint accuracy, when the lights went out. Billy Ray Smith, the Baltimore tackle, had creased me right across the bridge of the nose, right where the double bar would have been. There was nothing dirty about it. Billy Ray had given me a clean lick, a forearm, the first of several thousand I was to get. I was almost completely out. They had to haul me off the field. They poured me onto the bench the way you'd pour a can of heavy oil, and they put cold towels across my face. I was lying there still wondering what country I was in when Van Brocklin came over and said in that inimitable style of his: "Welcome to the National Football League, kid!"

By half-time I'd recovered my wits enough to ask Stubby Eason to put a double bar on my helmet, but I didn't play any more that day, and I didn't complain about it, either. I stayed on the bench in the next game, too, nursing my sore face and studying the action, trying to figure out how those pro quarterbacks kept from getting cotton-ginned out there.

One thought never entered my mind, believe it or not, and that is that I didn't have the stuff for the NFL. Maybe this just showed that I didn't understand the situation. Here I was fresh out of college, young and ignorant, and my total pro career consisted of getting lucky on one pass play in the first exhibition game, getting in for one whole play in the second game, and sitting out the third. And yet I never questioned myself or my potential. It is just not part of my philosophy to question myself or to think negatively. I try to leave that sort of thinking to others.

And don't think there weren't plenty of pro experts who thought negatively about me. The mere fact that I wasn't drafted till the third round tells you something, doesn't it? That really hurt my pride. That told me there were plenty of guys around who weren't the least bit impressed by my record at Georgia, where I was AP All-American in my senior year. I figured I knew my job, and my job was T-formation quarterback, and the pros should be hot after me. When the first two rounds went by and I was still standing there with an empty dance card, I had to reassess my thinking. I knew what was bothering the pro scouts, but I also knew that they were wrong.

You see, my first choice in sports had been baseball. All through high school I had dreamed of becoming a major league pitcher, and then in my junior year I was pitching against Willie Moore, a tough hitter on the Covington (Georgia) High School team, and I tried to give the ball a little extra spin and I felt a snap. A tendon had given way just below my right elbow, and that ended my pitching career. I couldn't even play shortstop after that, the long throw from the hole was too much for me. But the strange thing was I could throw a football just as high and hard as ever! For some freakish physiological reason, the tendon I had wrecked played no part at all in throwing a football. I don't know the medical explanation either.

But when those pro scouts study you, they study you, and when they find out that you wrecked a tendon throwing a baseball in high school, they've got to look at you as a risky draft choice. Never mind that I had enjoyed a thoroughly successful career as a T-quarterback under Wally Butts — the feeling still lingered that there was a fatal flaw in my physical structure, and sooner or later it would show up. The fact that I had asthma didn't help, either, or that I was a minister's son, and ministers' sons are supposed to be too nice to run anything as hard-nosed as a pro football team. (Whoever started that idea doesn't know ministers' sons!)

The scouts were doubtful about my small size and my ability to throw the long ball, which goes to show that even the experts have some funny ideas about professional football skills. Not that I have one of the superstrong arms in the NFL; I don't. But you don't need a super-arm, and a lot the pro scouts still don't realize that. The fact is that the home run is the easiest to throw, from the standpoint of pure muscle. It takes more strain to throw a 20-yard pass down the sidelines than it does a long ball. You have to throw the short ball hard, on a line, whereas the long ball is kind of looped into the air.

And still the pro scouts go out and beat the bushes for big, strong quarterbacks, guys with super-arms. Some of them are in the league now. Players like Rudy Bukich, Roman Gabriel, and Zeke Bratkowski can throw the ball 60 yards almost on a line and 70 or 80 yards with an arch. I've never had this kind of strength, and neither have most other NFL quarterbacks. Bart Starr doesn't have a super-arm, he's just a great passer. But the big muscle excites the scouts, just the same as a man who can run the 100 in 9.5 gets them all het up, thrills them to death. They're out there looking for the long bomber and it's the most overestimated talent in quarterbacking.

Well, I sulked and brooded and questioned the intelligence of the pro football establishment after it took three rounds for me to be drafted. The Vikings were offering me a $16,000 package, which was just about the going rate in those Neanderthal days before Joe Namath, Donnie Anderson, O. J. Simpson, and all those other nouveau riche kids on the block. The Boston Patriots offered $5,000 more. For me, there was no choice. I pride myself on trying to be businesslike, but there was no doubt that the AFL was the inferior league, and I wanted to show everybody that I could make it with the big guys. I didn't figure it would prove anything if I went to the AFL; the new league had been going for a year and it was still a humpty-dumpty operation. So I accepted the Minnesota offer and flew up to Minneapolis for a talk with Van Brocklin.

The club had never played a game, but they had their quarterback situation all figured out. They had wanted a veteran, and they had had a choice of Bill Wade of the Los Angeles Rams, Y. A. Tittle of the San Francisco 49ers, or George Shaw of the New York Giants. Shaw was then 27 years old and had been alternate quarterback to Charley Conerly during those years when New York was mowing everybody down. The Vikings figured George could be a great quarterback on his own if he could ever get out from under the shadow of Conerly, so they grabbed him. "There won't be a lot of pressure on you," Van Brocklin told me in that first meeting, "because there's no doubt about who our starting quarterback is. George is a seasoned professional, he's got all the tools, and we'll play him and bring you along nice and slow, let you learn your trade."

I didn't like that, I didn't like that one bit. Maybe Van Brocklin thought it was in my best interest to be brought along slowly, but I figured I could play in the pros even as a rookie. And that's the attitude I took to camp with me.

After a week of training camp the thought flickered through my mind that maybe I was in a little deeper water than I had expected. I didn't ever think that I wouldn't make it, not for one second, not then or any other time, but I did begin to realize that I wasn't playing with a bunch of Bloomer Girls either. We'd had a good draft that year, an excellent draft handled by Joe Thomas and Bert Rose, and guys like Ed Sharockman, Tommy Mason, and Rip Hawkins had come into camp. And we had some great old pros that year. We had Hugh McElhenny from the 49ers. Until Gale Sayers came along I would say that Hugh McElhenny was the greatest halfback in the history of the game, and I still would not rate

Sayers over him. And we had Mel Triplett from New York, with that stutter change-of-pace running style, Don Joyce, the great defensive end from the Colts, Bill Bishop, the fine tackle from the Bears, and Bob Schnelker, the big graceful end from the Giants — all of them 10-year veterans. When you'd worked out with players like that, you realized how far you were from Broad and Lumpkin Streets in Athens, Georgia.

One day early in the training season, Van Brocklin was watching me throw passes along the sidelines. I was lobbing them 50 yards, high and fat and soft. I prided myself on the fact that a 12-year-old kid could catch my long passes. "Hey, Peach, come over here!" Van Brocklin ordered. I walked over expecting a compliment on my featherlike parabolic passes, but instead he announced loudly that if I kept on passing like that I would be run right out of the league. "You've got to zip the ball!" he said. He ordered me to lift a five-pound dumbbell 25 times a day and work on throwing the ball in a flatter arc. "Maybe you're not used to the shape of the pro football yet," he said. "Here!" He handed me a pro ball, fatter in the middle than the college model, and told me to carry it at all times till I got used to the feel of it. That made me feel like a kid in kindergarten, carrying a football with me wherever I went, to learn its size. It was a badge of ignorance. *See the football. See how it's shaped. See how the*

*laces run down the middle. Now throw the foot-*
*ball. See how it wobbles. . . .*

Those preparations for our first regular season
in the NFL started me on a succession of feelings
of elation and depression in almost perfect rhythm.
If you charted my emotions in spring training,
it would look like the Himalayas. I came in
brimming with confidence, and then I discovered
I didn't even know how to throw a pro-type pass,
and I felt down in the dumps. Then my team
went out and beat George Shaw's team 35-7 in an
intra-squad game, and I was ready to join the
All-Pro squad. Then Billy Ray Smith knocked me
on my tail in the second exhibition game and I
was down in the dumps again. But it's not my
nature to stay down, and certainly not to give up.
I sat on the bench and learned a lot during the
third exhibition game, and by the time the fourth
game came along, against the Chicago Bears at
Cedar Rapids, Iowa, I had built my confidence
back up to the top. The Bears had a lot of those
bubble gum card guys too, but I wasn't going to
go out there and faint just because the other team
had some historic personages.

George Shaw started the game at quarterback,
but I took over in the second quarter. The Bears
had a murderous defense in those years — they
still do — and my previous 15 minutes or so of
exhibition game experience had not prepared me
for their blitzing defense. On one of the first plays

I called they threw an all-out blitz at us and this enabled Doug Atkins, 6'8" and 255 pounds, to get through the line untouched. Normally, he would have been picked up by our tackle, but the tackle had to block the first threat, a blitzing linebacker, and that left this diesel truck of a man headed for the pass-pocket at about 90 miles an hour. There's nobody there to block him except 195-pound Tommy Mason, himself a rookie, and Tommy goes low to cut Atkins down at the shoe tops, and Atkins hurdles right over Tommy! Tommy never touches him! And all I can see is this huge shape winging through the air at me, blotting out the sun, and then *crunch!* It sounded like a big old farm horse falling on a duck.

The Bears' corner linebacker, Larry Morris, is from Georgia Tech, the hated rival of my own University of Georgia Bulldogs, and all afternoon he would bust in on me, holler, "Hi Bulldog!" and slam me down. To this day, I flinch when somebody says "Hi Bulldog!" And Bill George and Joe Fortunato, the Bears' other linebackers, were knocking me around all afternoon. When it wasn't Fortunato, it was Morris, and when it wasn't Morris, it was Bill George, and when it wasn't Bill George, it was somebody else. And I didn't have the slightest idea what to do about it!

The Bears have always had a perplexing defensive style. They had about eight different defensive formations, and they still do. They're confusing right now to any veteran NFL quarterback. They give you a frightful learning problem. Let's say you have five bread-and-butter running plays. Okay, when you play the Bears you have to learn how to run each of these plays against eight different defenses. That's 40 plays. But a pro football team will usually go into a game with about 30 plays on its ready list, and if you want to execute perfectly against the Bears, you've got to know 240 routines, and that's just about 200 too many. The basic defensive philosophy of the Bears is to confuse, and this is the direct opposite of a team like Green Bay, whose philosophy is to let you know exactly how they're going to play and then out-execute you all the way. Of course, the complexity of the Bears' defense makes them vulnerable at a few points, too, but I wasn't experienced enough to know what these vulnerabilities were.

The Bears give up a lot of home runs, but not against rookie Fran Tarkenton on that black day in 1961. I was demoralized, panicky, and totally unsure of how to handle this team of blitzing dervishes. I'd come up to the line to call signals and I'd see the three linebackers cheating toward the line, all of them down in the three-point stance that spells "blitz!" So, I'd start to check off to another play, one that would work against the blitz, and the instant I'd start the audible the Bears would go into another formation, and then

41

I'd check back and they'd change to a blitzing formation.

Later on I learned that they were spotting the audibles by the expression on my face and the sound of my voice. And also by dead give-aways such as this one: I checked off to a play that would send the tight end out for a short pass, and I turned my head toward him as I called it, so he'd be sure not to miss the call! Wasn't that brilliant? By the time that poor tight end got out there to take the pass, the four defensive backs, two assistant coaches, and the lady who runs the Coke stand had him surrounded.

That game against the Bears marked the only time in my life that I was ever sort of hoping that the coach would take me out. But Van Brock-lin wouldn't do it. Evidently he wanted to see how I would react under fire. Well, I reacted poorly. I simply didn't know enough about pro quarterbacking, especially against a cute defense like Chicago's. It was a massacre. I was stepped on, tackled around the head, cut on the face, clothes-lined, and elbowed till my body was just one continuous bruise. From the knee down, my right leg was swollen to twice its size, and I still have a knot on it that stands out nearly an inch.

Worst of all, the Bears had beaten me mentally. I was completely down. I came away wondering if there was the slightest possibility that I could ever amount to anything in the National Football

League — if I really had a chance at all. I looked around me at the fellows on our own ball club and I felt awful at not measuring up, and I began to think that maybe pro football players were just different animals from me. I don't know why I didn't think of quitting right then and there, but I honestly didn't. Maybe I just couldn't believe that things could stay this black.

And then came the last game of the exhibition season against Los Angeles, and the whole erratic pattern of my rookie year continued. My graph went from Death Valley to the top of Mount Whitney in a single game. I didn't even get into the game till the third quarter, when we were losing by three touchdowns, but once I got in there, everything just went bam-bam-bam, right down the field, every play a jewel. We scored two touchdowns and came within a few yards of winning the game, and I was saying to myself, "See, boy? It's not so hard after all! You can do it! You belong here!"

There was one play when we cut McElhenny loose and he ran for about 50 yards and came back to the huddle with his tongue hanging out like a chow dog in Bessemer, Alabama. "Kid," he said in the huddle, "don't call my play this time. I'm tired!" Well, what was I going to do about that? Here's a guy who has always been a legend to me, a face on a bubble gum card, and right in front of all the other players he tells me not to call his number. Do you let him have his way or do you run him again? I ran him again, and he made another nice gain, and he looked daggers at me. But later on we laughed about it, and I found out that he had gone to Van Brocklin and told him the whole story and said, "When that kid called my play the second time, I knew we had a quarterback!"

After that game, Van Brocklin took me aside and told me I had won the starting job against the Bears in the first regular-season game the Minnesota Vikings would ever play. I was going to be the *charter* quarterback. I was shocked and I was thrilled to death. That night my wife, Elaine, and I went over to the Van Brocklins and had dinner with him and his wife, Gloria, and I was up on cloud 64, listening to one of the greatest quarterbacks in pro history talk to me as one great quarterback to another, as though I was a peer. "Look at this house, Peach," Van Brocklin said, and he showed us around his beautiful home in the suburbs of Minneapolis. "Pro football has done all this for me. We've got this nice home, we've got two cars in the garage, and if you work hard you can have the same."

We rolled some films of the Bears' games and talked over some strategy, and around midnight Elaine and I went home. I had plenty to think about: preparing to take the newest franchise in pro football into battle against the oldest, getting ready to play against the team that had maimed me just two weeks before. But in the glow of being accepted as a starting quarterback in the National Football League, I slept the sleep of a baby. A few days later, on a Friday before the game, Van Brocklin took me aside and said, "Francis, I'm not gonna start you Sunday. I feel I owe it to George Shaw to give him a crack at it. He didn't have a good exhibition season, but that isn't what counts. We haven't lost any regular-season games with him, and I've got to let him play till we do."

At first I was really hurt, really flabbergasted. I felt that I had competed with George for the first-string quarterback job, and I had won the decision. But later I got to thinking how George was a six-year NFL veteran, how the Vikings had given away their first draft choice to get him, and how he deserved a chance to show what he could do when the games counted. I realized all that, but it didn't keep me from severe internal bleeding, mostly around the pride area.

I have never studied so hard for anything in my life as I did for that Bear game. I knew I wasn't starting, but I also knew I had every chance of getting into the game, and I wanted to atone for that awful performance against the Bears in the exhibition season. In that game I hadn't known what to expect, but for the regular season opener I learned the Bear defenses thoroughly, how to recognize them instantly, and, most important, how to attack each one of them. And Van Brocklin came up with a brilliant game plan. His idea was to have a few plays to run against each defense, based on the inherent weakness in each defense. Then, after we had beaten each of their radical defensive setups, they would stop being so cute and settle down to a pretty honest defense, at which time we would also settle into a pretty honest offense. In other words, we would be just as cute as they were, and when they stopped being cute, *we'd* stop being cute. Of course, the whole plan was based on our quarterback's being able to read the Chicago defense in the first place.

Well, George Shaw started, and we kicked one field goal and missed another. On the third series of downs Van Brocklin sent me in. I hadn't called two plays before I realized the value of study, of poring over scouting reports and squinting at movies, and working up probability charts till your eyeballs ache. Two weeks before, in the exhibition game, I would look at the Bears' defensive alignment and it would be as incomprehensible to me as Sanskrit. But now, after studying the Bears night and day for a week, I would charge up to the line of scrimmage and recognize what they were up to. Well, not every time, no. There's not a quarterback in the league, even today, who can read those Bears any too clearly. But I did sniff out their defenses well enough so that they soon found it unprofitable to use most of their trickier stuff, and, just as Van Brocklin had predicted, they settled into an honest defense. But by then it was too late. It was just one of those days when I couldn't miss. I thought I was Sammy Baugh out there! Everything fell into place, all those lessons of the past two months. The final stats showed 17 completions in 23 attempts for 250 yards. I completed four touchdown passes, I ran for another score, and we beat the Bears 37-13. We were tied for first place in the National Football League, and I had the game ball from my debut in the big league.

Well, that was a taste of honey for me and the new ball club. We developed a false sense of well-being. Or I did, anyway. I figured we'd never lose a football game for the rest of our lives, least of all to those rinkydink Dallas Cowboys that we were playing in our second game. They were only a year older than we were, and *we* had just beaten the Bears. So we went to Dallas all full of confidence — and lost 21-7. Our team played pretty well. We were on their half-foot line almost at the end of the game when we fumbled. But I, personally, played a lousy game. Maybe I had read too many of my press clippings, or maybe I had exhausted myself mentally getting ready for the Chicago game. That's what I told myself. But the real truth was that one thing had caught up with me: I was a rookie, that's all, and I just plain didn't know enough. There was nothing complicated about it.

When I look back now and realize how little I knew in that first year in the pros, it scares me to death! It's a wonder I wasn't killed. It's a wonder we beat anybody. But we did. In our ninth game of the season, we played Baltimore in Minneapolis and beat the Colts 28-20. And that was the great Baltimore team, the championship team, with Johnny Unitas, Ordell Braase, Gino Marchetti, Lenny Moore, Raymond Berry, the whole cast of thousands, and all of them in their prime. And then we beat the Rams 45-21 for a grand total of three victories out of 14 games, which is three more than the Cowboys had won in their maiden season the year before. So, all in all, it wasn't a bad start.

Of course, to be perfectly honest, those victories were just little islands of satisfaction in a wide sea of frustration. After beating Chicago in the opener, we lost nine straight, and it got pretty nerve-racking around the locker room. I'd come home at night so upset that I couldn't talk. I knew I could play better, perform better, and yet I wasn't. I just plain didn't realize how little I knew. I didn't look at myself as a rookie quarterback. After all, I had been a quarterback one place or another for about ten years, and I figured I should be able to perform like Otto Graham.

It makes me laugh nowadays when I look back

on my ignorance. I'd do things like never taking my eyes off my primary receiver. Can you imagine anything so naïve? I'd make up my mind I was going to throw to so-and-so and I'd look at nobody else, and by the time I'd release the ball, he'd be surrounded. The free safety would always be on him, and sometimes a linebacker or two along with the cornerback. So I had to learn (it all seems so elementary now) that the defensive secondary watches the movement of the quarterback's eyes and head, and before you have any chance whatsoever to complete a deep pass, you've got to "look" the free safety off, stare at some other point on the field to attract him there, and not throw the ball till your receiver is in nothing worse than a one-on-one situation.

I could write a book on the mistakes I made, and it would run to about 600 pages, and it would never repeat the same mistake twice. Like the way I used to drop back one way when I was going to throw a short, flare pass, and drop back an entirely different way on a deep pass. I might just as well have gone into the pocket shouting, "Deep pass! Deep pass!" It was *that* obvious. I had to learn to make my moves in exactly the same way under all conditions, just as a baseball pitcher must use the same motion whatever he's throwing. I'm not saying I've perfected my moves yet. You're always learning in the pros. But, in that first year, everybody could tell what I was up to. I was being read by more people than Margaret Mitchell.

And sometimes I thought I would never learn how to conceal my audibles, or how to sound exactly the same at the line of scrimmage no matter what type of play I was calling. Those old pros like Joe Schmidt of the Detroit Lions would know what I was going to do before I did it. I think the low point of my intellectual career came in a game against the Lions, with Schmidt, the middle linebacker, calling defensive signals against us. All during the game he was shifting the defenses around to match my calls. Finally there was one play where I checked off three times and Schmidt changed the defense three times, and I got so frustrated I just called for time. I felt better later when I learned that the Cowboys' fine quarterback, Don Meredith, had been caught in a similar predicament against the New York Giants and instead of calling for time, he just threw his hands in the air and hollered, "Aw, ——!"

Through all of those agonies, I still kept thinking of myself as a fortunate fellow. In the whole history of the pros, there have been only three or four quarterbacks who broke into the starting lineups in their first year and stuck. Frank Ryan, the Cleveland Browns' quarterback, has said that I was lucky to get to play right away, and I agree with him. On the other hand, a young quarterback can be broken by the pressure if he doesn't keep a tight emotional hold on himself. I can think of one NFL quarterback who came into the league as a starter and it ruined him. He had everything, too, and yet he never had a really good year. The strain got him; he lost his confidence. There have been others who broke down in that rookie year under the pressure and the thrusts of playing and losing, playing and losing, week after bloody week.

Me, I didn't have enough sense to break down. I figured it was an advantage, in the long run, to play on a new-franchise team. We didn't have the personnel; we didn't have the experience. Very few of my teammates had top ability, and neither did I. But we had the advantage of going through every tough situation together. Nobody got any false idea that it was easy. When it came to the bedrock of pro football, suffering and hurting, making mistakes, taking licks, getting knocked down and jumping up so you could get knocked down again, we Minnesota Vikings led the league.

# 3

In some ways a pro quarterback's second year is the hardest. He has picked up a little learning, just enough to place himself in mortal peril. He hasn't matured yet — and he won't for two or three more years — but he goes around saying to himself, "Oh, boy, I've got it! I'm a veteran!" So he goes out there on the field with his head held high, his shoulders squared, and gets knocked on his backside and his team loses 47-7.

Let's not beat around the bush: We had a lousy second year at Minnesota, the worst year in the team's history, and I've got to take the blame. I'm not trying to beat my breast and say *mea culpa* and oh what a poor old martyr am I, not at all. *Every* pro football player takes defeat very hard, and I'm no exception. *Every* pro football player can look back on each loss and see where there was some little thing he could have done that might have changed the direction of the whole game. This is especially true of quarterbacks and especially true of me. I can show you the game film of every game I've ever lost and point out key mistakes I made. And if you don't thoroughly understand the nature of the pro game, you're likely to sit there and watch the films and say, "Yeh, but look at the mistakes the other guys on your team made. Look how many points your defensive team let in!" And my answer to that may sound corny, but it is nevertheless true: That pro football is a team game in every respect, and when one part of the team is having a bad day, the other part of the team is supposed to step in and pick them up. If the defensive team allows 50 points, my job is to get 51. I know the defensive players feel the same way about their job. If I can't put more than seven points on the scoreboard for our team, then it's their job to hold the other team to six. From a strictly objective, dispassionate point of view, there might be holes in this logic, but football isn't played from a strictly objective, dispassionate point of view. It is a highly emotional affair, and every player feels personally guilty about every loss.

Viewed entirely from my spot at quarterback, I had to feel like the world's biggest failure in that 1962 season. I'd spent the whole off-season reading all the gaudy newspaper stuff about me, and I was too young to put this in perspective. I became convinced that we were going to wreck the rest of the league in our second season in existence. Then we went out and won a grand total of two games — that's right, two games! — and tied one and lost eleven. Our offense wasn't completely inept — we lost games like 31-30 to the Bears and 39-31 to the Steelers in successive weeks — but some of the figures can be deceptive. For example, although I completed less than 50 per cent of my passes (49.5 per cent) for the first and only time in my career, which looks bad, I did throw 22 touchdown passes, which looks good — until you realize that many of them were desperation passes thrown when we were out of the ball game. A desperate team is going to score home runs, but not much else.

In some ways, becoming a mature pro quarterback is like joining a fraternity — there's a certain amount of hazing you just have to go through. Mine started in that miserable second year. I remember one time when I was having a bad day and the fans began to ride me. First there was this low undercurrent of boos, and then, for the first time in my pro career, I began to hear things like "Get him out of there!" and "We want McCormick! We want McCormick!" (John McCormick was the back-up quarterback; George Shaw hadn't made the team that year.) So pretty soon Van Brocklin took me out, and I don't blame him. He put McCormick in, not in response to the crowd, but because I was playing like Edna St. Vincent Millay out there.

It's a lonesome walk to the sidelines, especially when thousands of people are cheering your replacement. It was the first time I'd ever been taken out of a pro game solely because of incompetence, and I wanted to find a place to hide. As I got to the sidelines, old Hugh McElhenny came out and put his arm around me in front of everybody. "Well, kid," he said, "you've arrived! You're now an NFL quarterback. They've booed you and you've been replaced. Welcome to the club!"

That was the first time I was ever booed with any degree of unanimity, but later on it happened plenty of times, and I just had to learn to let it bounce right off me, to keep reminding myself that every quarterback gets booed. I've heard Unitas booed, and Bill Wade, John Brodie, and Charley Johnson. We're all booed, sometimes even when we deserve it. This is part of the life of a quarterback. And don't kid yourself: You hear it! Those cool characters who go around saying they don't hear the booing or the cheering are trying to kid somebody, maybe themselves. You hear boos and you hear cheers. There's nothing that animates me like a live crowd, a very enthusiastic crowd. The whole place is alive, full of electricity, and you feel that force coming down out of the stands and enveloping you. For the most part, the fans up at Minnesota were on the restrained side. They're wonderful fans, wonderful people, but they don't generate the electricity that crackles around you in stadiums like Dallas, Baltimore, New York, Atlanta, Green Bay, and a few other places.

A quarterback can feel this current, even when it's going against him, and he's got to understand it and put it to his own good use. He can't be oversensitive. He's got to realize that everybody in those stands is a quarterback. There are no middle linebackers in attendance, no flankers. They're all quarterbacks, even the old ladies. I'm the same way myself. When I'm watching a football game I'm the super quarterback in the sky. I think I know everything, sitting up there with my ticket stub in my pocket, and I say to myself, "Why'd he do that? He had three men open and he throws to the one guy who's covered!" That's the inalienable right of every spectator, to know everything. When you get down on the field, you discover that there are one or two things you don't know. When you lose that puppeteer's view of things, the whole perspective changes.

But in 1962 I was only 22 years old, a fresh kid from Athens, Georgia, and I didn't fully understand why all the fans didn't love me and my work. I had to have some sense knocked into me. In fact, in the last game of that worst-ever season, I had a *lot* of sense knocked into me. I was skipping down the sidelines past several pursuing Baltimore Colts when suddenly I was all alone in a dark room, naked and afraid and looking for the light switch. Wendell Harris, a 180-pound defensive back, had given me the old clothesline and knocked me out.

It's a funny thing: I have been knocked out twice in my career, and both times it was by one of those defensive backs, the only guys in the pro game who are smaller than I am. The other one was Dave Whitsell of the Bears, and he nailed me in 1963, the Bears' championship year, when they were rolling over everybody in sight. On the third play of the game, I tucked the ball under my arm and took off on a run, and while I was looking sideways at several other players, Whitsell clotheslined me at full speed and I mean I was really out! They carried me off the field and I came to in slow stages. In the first stage, I sat up and took a place on the bench, even though I was still unconscious. In the second stage, I conversed with my teammates, and to this day I don't remember a word I said. I didn't actually come to until there were only four minutes left in the first half. It was like waking up from a dream, feeling myself sitting on the bench, hearing myself talking to my buddies, and not even knowing where I was. President Kennedy had been assassinated the week before, and that was the first thing that hit my mind as I groped my way out of the fog. I needed some fixed point, something to relate to, so I ran over to the team doctor, Dr. Don Lannin, and I said, "Didn't the President get killed? Didn't the President get killed?" I hoped he'd say no, and then I'd know I was in a dream and, when I woke up, President Kennedy would still be alive. But he said, "Yes, he did, Fran." And then I realized where I was and who I was.

In the third year of the new franchise, we won five games and we did a lot of things better, but I was still immature. It wasn't till the next year that I felt that I was beginning to be a genuine, bona fide professional quarterback, able to react properly to the pressures of the game. That's the dominating factor about pro football, the pressure, and you can't stay around if you can't handle it. You may beat the Chicago Bears one Sunday and the very next Sunday you've got Detroit with Alex Karras and Roger Brown coming at you, and just seven days after that Green Bay is coming in with Willie Davis after your hide. Now this is tough, but if it's going to bother you, you don't belong in the pros as a quarterback. The quarterback has to learn that he gets too much blame for the losses and he gets too much credit for the wins, but that's the job he signed on to do, he's well paid for it, and he'd better accept it.

Even when we lost at Minnesota, I felt we were learning something. I felt we were headed slowly but surely for the divisional championship, improving with each game, making fewer mistakes, learning our jobs. And the 1964 season seemed to bear me out. Baltimore won the Western Division championship that year, and one of the only two games the Colts lost all season was to the Vikings. It was the season opener, a classic football game that made me realize what potential we had on our team. We finished the season with eight wins, one tie, and five losses, and tied with Green Bay for second place in the division. We led the NFL in total offense with 4,800 yards, and that year five Minnesota offensive players were selected for the Pro Bowl: Center Mick Tingelhoff, Tackle Grady Alderman, and Backs Bill Brown, Tommy Mason, and me.

So the stage was set for 1965, our fifth year in the league, and for the first time people began to pick us for the division title. Around Minnesota, there was no doubt about it: The Vikings were a cinch to win. We even got the nod from some less biased observers. *Sports Illustrated* picked us to finish second, and gave us a shot at the title. Several national columnists were just as high on us.

So what happened? Well, in simple English, we blew it, that's all. We started the season like a horde of Mongols and we finished the season like the Ladies' Auxiliary of the West Augusta Gladiola Club.

Our exhibition season consisted of five games and five wins. In the next-to-last game of the preseason schedule, we creamed Dallas 56-7, and if you think that Dallas was any lily of the valley that year, let me remind you that *Sports Illustrated* had picked the Cowboys to win it all, and with plenty of justification.

En route to Baltimore for the opener, it was just as though we were on the way to the championship game. We were all geared up, high as hooty owls. Phil King said to me that he'd never seen a football team as ready as we were, and he'd never felt a pressure, an intensity, like this even in his days on the championship teams at New York. We hit the field at Baltimore like the 3rd Division coming ashore at Anzio. The temperature was 94, the hottest September 19 in Baltimore in 70 years. With Baltimore's waterfront humidity, it felt like 124 out there, but we didn't care. We had been practicing all summer in cool weather in Bemidji, Minnesota, but we were so ready that we didn't figure anything could stop us, least of all the weatherman. Baltimore had been working out all week in this heat, so the Colts were somewhat accustomed to it.

The first time the Colts got the ball, our defense intercepted a Unitas pass. Our offensive team was out on the field like a bunch of Olympic sprinters and on the first play I hit Hal Bedsole for a touchdown. It was 7-zip, and the late arrivals were still coming into the stadium! I told you we were ready!

And then it reached us. The first quarter wasn't even over when I was sitting on the bench between Bill Brown and Tommy Mason and I noticed that both of them were gulping for air as though they had just picked an acre of cotton. Out on the field our left guard almost passed out and had to be yanked. With less physical exertion than anybody (and I'm from Georgia and presumably accustomed to heat), I was so exhausted I could hardly make it back onto the field. And we still had three quarters to play!

Well, we had a lousy day, especially me, and we lost 35-16. I'm not saying that the Baltimore players didn't do a great job against us, because they did, and they deserved to win all the way. But I *am* suggesting that they were a little better adjusted to that heat than we were, just as we were usually a little better adjusted to extreme cold when we played home against other ball clubs. Over the long pull, weather advantages tend to even out, but that didn't alter the fact that we had gone into Baltimore loaded for bear and had blown the opener in what was supposed to be the start of our big run at the title. I can't describe the psychological effects of that loss. But the second week was even worse, because this time we had no weather problem to blame, we had only ourselves.

We were ahead of the Detroit Lions 29-24 with 30 seconds to go in that second game, and they were on the 48-yard line. So I was sitting on the bench feeling pretty good about the whole thing. Detroit only had time for a couple more plays, and their quarterback, Milton Plum, who is anything but a big scrambler, went back to throw, broke out of the pocket, danced around, and finally lofted a long desperation pass in the general direction of Amos Marsh. Marsh caught the ball over his shoulder 48 yards away and squarely between two defenders. He's never caught a ball like that before in his life, and with 20 seconds left on the clock we were dead. The team that was going to blow everybody down now had gone 0 for 2!

To the everlasting credit of my teammates at Minnesota, we pulled up our socks and won some ball games after that, but you just cannot appreciate the effect of that poor start on a team as keyed up as we were. To lose your first two games means that you automatically become an extreme long shot as far as winning the division is concerned. The season before that, Baltimore had won in the West and had only lost two games *all year*. In many ways, I think that the Minnesota Vikings' finest hour came in the weeks after we lost those two games. A lesser group of men would have folded. But we went out to Los Angeles to play in 95-degree heat, and this time we arrived five days before the game instead of the day before, and we won on a long touchdown drive in the last two minutes, 38-35.

We won the next game and then we got hit with another one of those key plays that can turn a season all around. Every contending ball club can look back on three or four catastrophic plays every year: The great teams go on and win anyway, the others never fully recover. We were paying the Chicago Bears, and we had gone ahead by six points after a long, sustained march against the clock. Now there were two and a half minutes left to play. Fred Cox kicked off to Gale Sayers, and all Sayers did was run it back 96 yards for a touchdown. You can imagine the scene in our locker room. All that was lacking was Chopin's *Funeral March!*

And yet our players didn't fold. We went out and beat San Francisco and then Cleveland, the 1964 champs, one of three games the Browns lost all year. We were right back in contention with a 4-3 record when we came up against the Baltimore Colts for a second time. Just before the game, we found out how the breaks can even up. The very same Baltimore team that had beaten us in the heartbreaking opener was now going to have to play us without their first-string quarterback, John Unitas. Gary Cuozzo was filling in for the injured Unitas, and everybody knows that back-up quarterbacks aren't supposed to win in the NFL. We went out and scored first, and it looked like an easy day. But the Colts got a field goal and then Cuozzo hit Jimmy Orr from 43 yards out and Baltimore scored. The half ended with us behind 10-7. We outplayed them 16 first-downs to three, and we were behind.

The great play of that ball game, another one of those key plays you look back on, came in the second half, and the man who made the call ought to be handed a lifetime appointment to The Institute for Advanced Study at Princeton. Both teams had scored, and it was one of those alternating propositions where no club gets very far ahead of the other and everybody begins to sense that the stronger team is going to pull it out by sheer endurance in the last quarter. Naturally, we hoped that was going to be us: The Colts and their alternate quarterback couldn't keep up such a sensational pace for the whole ball game. Then the Colts scored and went ahead of us 24-14, but there was still plenty of time for us to come back. Our offensive team jumped up, ready for the kick-off after the Colts' extra point, and instead Baltimore kicked an onside kick, recovered it, and scored again! For my money, that onside kick was the play of the year. Who in the world kicks onside with a 24-14 lead?

Baltimore's strategic geniuses had assessed the

situation beautifully. They knew we had a tough offense and they knew we were ready to roll. Their 10-point lead looked anything but safe. But if they could keep the ball away from our offense, their 10-point lead looked good. And if they could score again . . . It was brilliant, and now the game was out of reach. Cuozzo wound up throwing five scoring passes, and we wound up out of contention for the divisional title. I can tell you: None of us felt good about losing the rematch to the Colts. That night we were all in a state of depression, really down. But on the other hand we weren't quite prepared for the jolt we got the next day, either.

I was sitting in a friend's office in Minneapolis on Monday when somebody came running in all out of breath and told us that Van Brocklin had quit. The coach had announced that he had brought the Vikings as far as he could bring them, that there were compelling personal reasons for his resignation, including the fact that he wanted to spend more time with his family, and that he was through as of now. I was shocked! At lunch, I got a call to go out to the home of Jim Finks, the team's general manager. Rip Hawkins, our defensive captain, rode out with me. It was a pretty grim group that waited for us at Jim's house. There were Jim and two directors of the club, Max Winter and Bernie Ridder, and all of them wanted Rip and me to talk Norm out of quitting.

I said, "As far as I'm concerned, I can't do it. Norm has said very clearly that he has thought it all out and made his decision for very good, personal reasons. I can't be selfish and go out there and tell him to override all his personal reasons and come back to the football team." Rip said he felt the same, and we both were pretty sure we were expressing the sentiments of the squad.

So that's where the matter stood till Tuesday morning, when we were scheduled to have our regular team meeting. To our great surprise, Norm showed up, expressed his apologies, and told us he was resuming his post as coach. After the meeting we were a pretty confused bunch of football players. We went out and practiced, but we looked like the "B" team of the Jones Jr. High in Toledo. We had a *terrible* week of practice, the worst ever. Then we had a team meeting, just Rip and me and the other players, and I said, "Look, regardless of what you may be thinking, this is *our* football team. It's what *we* make of it. And if we go out and play poorly on Sunday it's not gonna reflect on anybody but us." Well, we went out and lost big on Sunday.

I tell you, that whole situation was awkward for everybody. It was tough on Norm and tough on us, and tough on the fans and tough on the owners. Morale was just plain shot. We lost four games and finished the season on a very confused note with a record of 7-7. In our big year, the year we were supposed to win everything, we wound up fifth, a derelict of a football team.

It would be nice to say that we all pulled up our socks and came roaring back in 1966 and had a great year, a year that made us forget the miseries of the season before. But the new season was even worse than the old. Oh, we had our moments, but they were widely spaced. We beat Green Bay once and surprised everybody, but certain other teams beat us and surprised everybody, too. And as the season wore on, I began to feel a great personal disenchantment. One by one, I was accumulating a full set of compelling, personal reasons of my own for leaving the team. And, finally, toward the end of the season, I decided that this would be my last year at Minnesota. It had become completely clear that my departure would be in the best interests of my teammates and myself.

I began planning how to tell Norm without causing any hard feelings, because I hate scenes and I hate hard feelings. I had more or less decided on going to his office, telling him how grateful I was for all he had taught me and how there was nothing personal about it but I just couldn't see my way clear to returning for the 1967 season. I was polishing the rough edges of my farewell speech when somebody told me that Van Brocklin wanted to see me in his office right away. It was the Tuesday after the Atlanta game, in the closing weeks of the season, and I hurried over. Norm looked upset, and I couldn't blame him. We were all living from one upset to another in those days. But I never expected what followed. "Francis," he said, "I'm quitting."

"You're quitting?" I said.

"I'm leaving this football team," he said.

I asked him if he was sure. He said he was, that he had already notified Jim Finks of his decision.

"Well," I said, "I wish you all the luck in the world, Norm, and I won't tell anybody else till you make the announcement." I groped around for what to say. The last thing I had expected was a Van Brocklin resignation. "Norm," I said finally, "it's a funny thing. I thought I was coming over here to tell you that I wasn't coming back."

He said, "No, Francis, you're the one who should be coming back. You're the life and heart of this team. You should stay, and with a few changes here and there, you can win a championship with this team."

I really had to admire Norm at that second. We had had our differences — we're both strong personalities, both stubborn cases in our own ways — and that was all the more reason for me to appreciate what he was saying. I knew it would have been a lot easier for him to hold back those words of praise.

I went out and had a quiet lunch with some

friends and said nothing about Van Brocklin's decision, and that afternoon there was another message for me to go to Norm's office. I hurried over to find him pacing the floor, excited, and charged up with energy. "Francis," he said when I walked in, "I really think I can still be a championship coach and you can still be a championship quarterback, the two of us, working together."

I didn't say a word. Once again he had taken me by complete surprise.

"I know that we kind of drifted apart this season" Norm went on, "and some of it's been my fault. We've gone through a lot together, and what I'd like to do more than anything is to wipe the slate completely clean, erase everything that's been said and done, and start over fresh and new."

Well, as I told you, I'm a pretty stubborn Georgia mule, but I'm also a sentimentalist, and that little speech of Van Brocklin's really touched me. The Minnesota Vikings were my life, my family. It was no easy thing to decide to leave them, to just lop off six years of my life, to leave behind a bunch of guys that I loved as much as I loved my own brother. I found myself looking for words again, for the second time that day. "Norm," I said at last, "there's nothing I'd like better."

He came over and gave me a big bear hug, and he wiped his eyes, and then we sat down and had one of the greatest talks of my life. We spent two hours planning what we would do to bring the championship of pro football to the Minnesota Vikings. We talked about the changes we would make, and the new outlook we would bring to the ball club. And when I left Norm's office that afternoon, I was right back in my old frame of mind. I figured there was nothing that could stop the Vikings now.

In a storybook, the happy ending would come next. Norm and I would work together like jewels and the team would win the championship of the world behind its fired-up quarterback and its dedicated coach. But it wasn't to be. We were two entirely different people, and only a day or two after our big reconciliation we were on the outs again. There's no point in going into the gory details. They're personal, and they're irrelevant. The fact of the matter is simply that it didn't work out. Give us credit: We both tried.

After the season, I went back to Atlanta and my off-season business interests, but I wasn't of much use to any of my associates. All kinds of thoughts were racing through my mind and they kept right on racing for six weeks, until one day I sat myself down and I said to myself: "Francis, you can't go back there and pretend that you agree with what's being done, and you can't change the way you feel. So you'll have to leave the Vikings and no more ifs, ands, or buts about it. Any other decision would be unfair to the coaches, the owners, the fans, and most of all to your fellow players."

That was a Saturday morning, and as the thought finished unreeling in my mind, I turned to Elaine and I said, "I'm not going back."

She said, "Whatever you want to do is fine with me."

That night I slept peacefully for the first time in months. I wasn't happy about my leaving, but at least I was finished with the weeks of indecision.

I had a speaking engagement in Spokane, and I routed myself through Minneapolis so I could stop off and tell Norm. We talked in his office for six hours and I told him that I was not coming back and that nothing would change my mind. We had a very pleasant conversation — we almost always did. As usual, we got sidetracked on the subject of what potential the Vikings had, what a wonderful bunch of guys they were, and how they deserved a division championship for all the sacrifices they had made. We went out to eat together, and then we went back to his office and talked some more, and I finally left late in the afternoon in a very confused state of mind. I wasn't confused about quitting, but I wasn't sure that Norm had accepted my resignation, or just how the matter stood. That's when I realized that the only way to do it was by letter. So I wrote:

Dear Norm,

After much thought, I have come to the definite conclusion that under no circumstances can I return to play football with the Minnesota Vikings next season.

Because of the events of the past few months and my feelings toward a number of things, it is impossible for me to return to the Vikings with a clear and open mind. As you know, I have tried to subdue these feelings and erase them from my mind, but it has been impossible.

Feeling as I do, I am sure that this decision is the best for the Vikings, you, and myself.

Norm, I sincerely appreciate your help and guidance during the early years of my pro career and I certainly wish for you, and the Vikings, every success.

I hope you and the organization understand that nothing can be done which would change my decision.

Because of all that the organization has done for me, I am writing this letter in the event that it might be helpful to the Vikings to know of my feelings at this time.

Sincerely,
Francis A. Tarkenton

I sent copies to all the directors and, as far as I was concerned, that was the end of the line. I'll

Caption for preceding photo: Even in training camp, the pressure is tremendous to "go all out." Here, in a scrimmage game against his teammates, Fran looks downfield for a receiver.

Fran gets ready to pass against Green Bay.

Fran can't scramble away from *this*
San Francisco 49er tackle.

Caption for preceding photos: Fran scrambles through Dallas defenders for a big gain. One look at the faces of the Cowboy defense tells the whole story.

Fran scrambles again behind perfect blocking.

Fran gets tackled by a Dallas defender
after a six-yard gain.

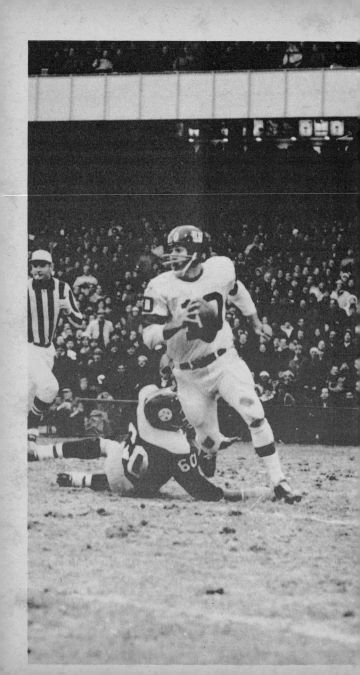

Left: As one Pittsburgh Steeler defenseman slips trying to nail him, Tarkenton prepares to throw way down field.

New York Giant Coach Allie Sherman chats with Fran on the sideline during a game against New Orleans.

With no danger in sight for yards around,
Fran carries the ball against St. Louis.

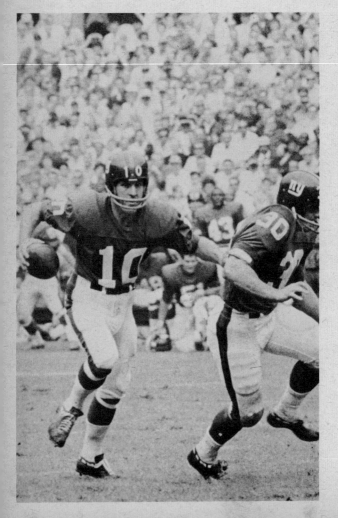

Will Fran hand off to Ernie Koy (No. 23), or will he scramble?

Here is Fran, last November, showing the
Dallas Cowboys some of the stuff that won
him "NFL Player of the Week" honors.
(New York won, 27-21)

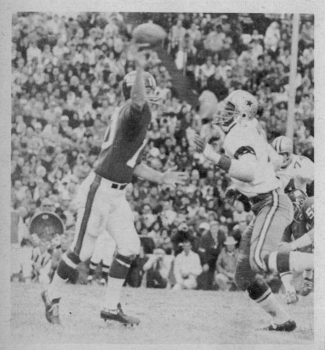

"The Scrambler" decides to pass, as two huge Washington Redskin defenders try to crash through.

Caption for preceding photos: As he follows his blocker, Fran looks far down field for an eligible receiver.

Pro football is rough on quarterbacks— even "scramblers." The huge tackle on the left almost seems to be knocking Fran down with one giant hand.

admit I was surprised when Van Brocklin resigned the day after he got my letter, but that didn't change anything I wrote. Once I had made up my mind, the decision was irrevocable. I wouldn't have been true to myself if I had reversed my field just because Van Brocklin had quit. My letter wasn't intended as a warlike act; it wasn't aimed at getting anybody. It was just a clear and simple statement of my position. If I'm an honorable man and I announce that I'm not coming back no matter what happens at Minnesota, how can I then turn around and rejoin the ball club? And if I do, how can I command the respect of anybody there, the directors, the fans, the popcorn vendors, let alone my fellow players?

But the trouble with simple English nowadays is that nobody believes it. When a politician says he will not run under any circumstances, he's right in there pitching in November. And when a baseball player says he's quitting the game, he's right back in action on opening day. So, naturally, after Van Brocklin left a lot of people assumed that I would come scampering back to the Vikings. I kept repeating that my letter had made it plain that I would not return under any circumstances, and I meant just that. Yes, they would say, but that was before Van Brocklin quit. That changed everything. I would say that Van Brocklin's resignation changed nothing, that I suffered from the unfortunate habit of saying what I mean and sticking by it.

As soon as people began to realize that I was not returning to the Vikings, an awful controversy began. I suppose, looking back on it, that the easy way out would have been to go on back and play out my years with Minnesota and try to be nice old Fran. But I just couldn't do that and be true to myself. The resulting uproar was disturbing; it broke into my life pattern; it upset me and my family. We had phone calls and crank letters. Sportscasters and reporters were calling us from all over the country, and it became a nuisance. I'd made my decision and it was over and I hadn't figured on any of this trouble. We were reading quotes out of Minneapolis papers about how ungrateful I was and things like that, and some of those remarks hit me like a slap in the mouth.

Worst of all, the shouting and the backbiting tarnished the finest thing that ever happened to me in my life: My association with the Minnesota football players. It was a happy association, I played with the finest men in the whole world, I made lifelong friends, and all this bitterness seemed profane to me after what we had gone through together on the field.

The thing about pro football is that it's a family affair, and I don't expect anybody who hasn't played the pro game to understand that completely. I've never seen a group of men with more love for one another than a pro football team. After the 1966 championship game an interviewer asked Vince Lombardi how his Green Bay Packer team was able to come up with so many great plays in the clutch, and Lombardi answered: "Because they have respect for one another. . . . They have a great deal of love for one another." He was speaking on network television, and I'll bet he confused a lot of the big, tough he-men around the country, talking about the Packers running on love. But they do. Every pro team does. I've never seen any place in the world, or any human activity, where love is more exemplified than on the pro football field. You go through so much together. There's the physical torture of training camp, where you give everything you've got to punish your body, to get yourself into shape for 14 weeks of war. And you watch your teammates get hurt, cut, broken. You watch them lose their jobs, you watch them go to the heights of victory together and the depths of despair together. You share every conceivable emotion. You watch their families grow, you're with them socially, and pretty soon your life is intimately bound up in theirs, and this intense love and devotion springs up.

It's funny: After a win you have the greatest feeling in the world, but the week after you lose a ball game you walk down the street and you feel like you don't have any friends. The writers are climbing on you and the sportscasters are jumping you and the people don't want your autograph. So where do you turn? You turn to the 40 guys who are still in there working and suffering with you; you can always depend on them.

That's why it's so hard to leave a team. It's tragic. The hardest thing about my leaving the Vikings was that for six years I played with those guys and I left a lot of my life in their keeping. Those guys are my family. They'll always be family to me.

# 4

When I was a kid I used to make up teams from bubble gum cards and stage football games on my bed. I'd go through my Philadelphia Eagle cards and study my personnel. There'd be Frank Kilroy and Vic Sears and Tommy Thompson, Bosh Pritchard and Steve Van Buren and Pete Pihos, and all the rest, and I'd try to figure out some kind of a game plan. It was based on what they did best, how well they had played in the previous games, how they had looked in the exhibition season, and the capabilities of the guys they were playing — who would usually be the Washington Redskins led by Bullet Bill Dudley. Oh, it was a very complex process. "Steve," I'd say to the Steve Van Buren bubble gum card, "we're going to be running you wide a lot today."

"Great, Coach," he would say, and I'd make a mental note for my game plan that Van Buren would carry the main load of the offense and that when I needed 10 yards I could always send him on an "end run."

Johnny Fullback had a slight charley horse, but nobody on the other team knew about it, so I figured that for short yardage we could always use him on a "center plunge." Bosh Pritchard had worked the "off tackle" play successfully the week before against the Chicago Bears. Tommy Thompson was having good luck with the buttonhook pass to Pete Pihos and once in a while he'd hit on a deep bomb to one of our deep men. So that would be my basic offensive game plan: The center plunge, end run, and off-tackle play, the short pass and the long pass, and for a little razzle-dazzle, I would include a Statue of Liberty play, an end-around, and a tricky tackle-eligible play. After all that planning, it was not surprising that my bubble gum Eagles were undefeated in my bedroom.

I did this from about the age of nine until I was 12 years old. I'd come home from school and run off those games till supper time, and then after supper I'd do it the rest of the evening. While the other kids were learning logarithms in the classroom, I was wondering how to use Pete Pihos this week. My studies suffered, but this was my interest, this was my life.

94

Well, it still is. And sometimes I wish my life had stayed as simple as it was in those dear dead days. Mostly, football was like a big shove-of-war. There were no flanker backs, no blitzes, and no 275-pound pass rushers who could step off the 100 in 10 flat. Life was sweet and pure and simple, and none of the quarterbacks had a Ph.D. from Rice. In those days the biggest problem was to execute. You knew how the other team's defense would set up every time. The problem was how to mix the plays and beat their static defense more often than they beat your static defense.

I'm not one of those quarterbacks who tries to impress the public with the complexities of running a modern pro-football offense. Everybody's job is more complex nowadays. Our whole society is vastly more complex, and the pro quarterback's job can be learned, piece by piece, just like everybody else's. You don't memorize the basic 300 plays overnight, and you're not expected to. And you don't learn how to read every other team's defenses until you've been around the league for four or five years, and even then you keep on learning new ones. But it is true that you can drive yourself batty trying to read defenses, figuring out how to beat them, adjusting to the time of the game, position on the field, the weather, the capabilities of your players, and the limitations of the opponents, and 134 other factors. As game time approaches each week, and all these problems come up anew, I go into more and more of a purple quandary trying to anticipate what's going to happen. By Friday or Saturday I'm running whole blocs of plays in my head, just like the bubble gum days. I'm trying to visualize every game situation, every defense, and how to beat it. I say to myself, "Now what am I going to do if I'm on their five-yard line and it's third and three and our short passing game hasn't been going very well, and it's misting?" I walk around on another planet, and I'm not much fun to live with.

I don't snap back at Elaine. Mostly I just don't hear her at all, and she's learned to adjust to it. A day or two before a game, she'll ask me what I'd like for dinner, and without really having heard her I'll say, "Oh, chicken, I guess," and soon you can smell the chicken cooking in the house, and then we'll sit down to dinner and Elaine'll say, "Here's your chicken, just the way you like it," and I'll take a bite, and I'll say, "What's this? Chicken?"

I spend whole nights thrashing around in bed playing the situations in advance, dreaming them in living color. The night before one of my games against Green Bay, I dreamed that we were first and goal on their nine-yard line. I've got three plays to get the ball into the end zone. And I've got to figure out what to call on first down against a defense that's been murdering me. The first play is the big play in the sequence; it determines everything that follows. If you run, you've got to run for at least five yards, otherwise you've committed yourself to nothing but passes from there on out. If you pass incomplete, you're also committed to nothing but passes. But if you pass or run for at least five yards, you've still got a free hand. And all these ideas are racing through my head in the dream, and the ball is on the right hash mark, and that limits us to certain plays, too, and doggone! Before I can pick a play and see how it all works out, I wake up! And I'm a son of a gun if the same identical situation doesn't come up the next day in the actual ball game: first and goal on the Green Bay nine from the right hash mark!

When I first came into the league in 1961, you could draw up your pass patterns with a reasonable expectancy of getting single man-to-man coverage or an occasional zone-type coverage, and that was all you had to worry about as far as pass defense was concerned. But nowadays they have a jillion different pass coverages to throw against you: single coverage, zone coverage, double coverage, combination coverage, weak side zones and sally zones, and who knows what all, and every one of them carefully camouflaged! As if that isn't bad enough, a lot of teams are beginning to play what is called "position on the field." Baltimore and Detroit started this and the rest of the teams are picking it up. In "position on the field," you zone the wide side of the field at all times, but if the offense is strong into the sideline, you use a double coverage strong side, a weak side zone to the wide side, and get them that way. There's a lot more to it, but basically the defense is determined by "position on the field," and you get a different concept, a more sophisticated concept, of defense.

If you've never played for a pro football team, you've got to wonder how in the world a quarterback can figure out all these things, especially when he has only a second or two in which to make his decision. He can study the defensive alignment as he is counting cadence, but the real decision has to be made when he is dropping back to pass, when the defensive ball players are on the move, and the true defense (in contrast to the camouflaged defense) is being tipped off.

Every quarterback has his own system of keys for reading defense. My own is to watch the middle linebacker and the strong side safety. By studying those two, I can usually tell what kind of pass coverage I'm up against. If the middle linebacker goes to the strong side, then I look for some type of single coverage, or maybe double, but at any rate I know it will be man-to-man. If he goes to the weak side, they're probably throwing a zone at me. If the strong safety goes back to a deep corner, that's going to be zone coverage, and if he stays up tight it's probably some sort of man-to-man. If the strong safety goes back to the middle, I'm going to expect a weak side zone. And so forth through the other possibilities. See how simple it is?

In the olden days of pro football, 10 and 12 years ago, you looked for other giveaways, like the way somebody positioned his feet. They used to say that the Eagles' quarterback, Tommy Thompson, would stand with his left foot forward when he was calling a running play and his feet parallel for a pass play. I don't know if that was true or not, but I do know that Tommy never committed that fatal error in my bubble gum games, or I'd have cut him from the squad and substituted Adrian Burk as fast as you could say "Dubble Bubble!" The big thing in those days was to come back to the huddle and say something like, "I've been watching that middle guard of theirs and when he's gonna rush the passer he keeps his left foot back an inch or two, so I'll tip you off when he does it and you can call a sweep. . . ." Football has become far too sophisticated for that sort of approach. In the first place, hardly anybody gives away free information anymore and, even if they did, you wouldn't have time to go around studying everybody's feet. You've got too much else to do.

This doesn't mean that you can't set up your offense to exploit some of the personal characteristics of the other team. I remember a game in my rookie year, 1961, when the problem was how to beat Night Train Lane, one of the best pass defenders in the game. Dave Middleton was an offensive end, and Dave was no slouch in the brains department (he's a doctor now), and he used to come back to the huddle and give me excellent advice. So after we'd run a few plays against Detroit, Dave said to me, "Look, Night Train's a gambler, and when he thinks he's got us in a bad spot he'll crowd right up on me, trying to get that interception on short passes, taking a chance we won't throw deep. So when that situation comes up, I'll tip you off."

Not long afterward, we were first and 10 on our own five-yard line, and Dave said, "Now!" So I called a play that would send Dave on an up pattern just running as fast as he could straight up the field. When we got to the line of scrimmage, sure enough, there was Night Train right on Dave's nose. I dropped back, set up in the pocket, looked at every possible receiver except Dave, and then let one go long and deep right down the middle. Dave had Night Train beaten by 10 yards and he caught the pass for a 50-yard gain. Night Train did a little less gambling for the rest of that game. But I don't mean to suggest that his gambling was a weakness. He was the most successful gambling-type defensive back I've ever played against, but every now and then you could beat him. Like once a season. . . .

Everything is changing so fast in pro football, sometimes even from week to week, that it's a full-time job keeping up with the new styles fresh from Chicago, Dallas, San Francisco, and every place else. If current trends keep up, I think you'll see less and less blitzing and fewer check-offs at the line of scrimmage. A lot of people think that check-offs, audibles, are the answer to cute defenses and fancy red dogging patterns, and once upon a time they were. In our second year at Minnesota, we carried the audible process to its ultimate against Los Angeles. We called every play audibly at the line without a huddle, at least till the Rams made certain adjustments. The problem was that we were hurting offensively — Tommy Mason was out and we had some other weaknesses — and the Los Angeles line was jumping around a lot, from four-three to five-three to five-two with all sorts of variations, and we were having an awful time figuring out an offense. So we decided to beat their defense by going right up to the line and calling an audible play on a short count. I'd say, "Set two 25 hut hut," and boom! the play was on. They didn't even have the time for a defensive huddle, let alone the time to do all that jumping around. We played this way for one entire quarter, or long enough to make them honest.

Nowadays the problem of shifting, switching defenses isn't solved by the audible so often. It's solved right in the huddle by giving the players flexible assignments. For example, suppose our tight end is to run a square-out pattern. In the old days, he'd probably have run that square-out pattern, period, and that would have been his whole assignment. But now he will run the pattern only if the linebacker on his side does not blitz. If the blitz is on, the tight end will block the blitzer. In other words, the possibility of a blitz is anticipated by the play. Of course, I've vastly oversimplified. When you figure that the tight end also will have a couple of other alternatives, you can begin to see how complex this new-type offense can get, especially when you realize that the tight end is only one of 11 players with choices and decisions to make after the ball is snapped.

The modern quarterback anticipates the probabilities and calls plays that will prepare his team for almost anything. He doesn't have to call audibles. Many times a good quarterback will go through an entire game without calling a single audible; his strategy against a tricky defense is built into his play-calling. And, anyway, an audible was never much more than a way to avert disaster. All you could do was go up there and check off and hope that everybody on your team caught the signal. A play is always better if it's called in the huddle. The quarterback who calls 10 or 12 audibles is becoming a thing of the past.

Another thing that is fading away is the blitz. NFL teams seldom use the blitz except against a young quarterback. If you try to blitz a veteran quarterback today points are going to go up on the scoreboard. What you do when you blitz is to put your defensive back in a man-to-man situation, with no help at all from the free safety, to cover a 9.3 sprinter who can go all over the field. No defensive back can cover a pass-catcher for more than a few seconds one-on-one, so the only way the blitz can be effective is if the quarterback is dumped right away.

Certain refinements have been introduced into the blitz, of course. What has happened in recent years is that linebackers have been taking more of a part in the coverage and they are changing their means of coverage. Essentially you've got seven men in the secondary now. Teams are going with four defensive linemen and bringing the safety in to play the weak-side linebacker in passing situations. The year before the Vikings put three defensive backs in linebacker positions in long-yardage situations, so that they could actually have seven defensive backs in the game at one time. That closes up the secondary pretty well. They don't mind if you run instead of pass, because you may get five, six, or eight yards but you're not going to get enough for the first down. Having so many agile players who can run so well means that you can do a lot of things on defense. Another refinement is that there are more and more safety blitzes, and in recent years we have been even blitzed by a cornerback, something I've never seen before. I don't even know what you'd call it — a cornerback blitz, I guess.

Although teams are doing a better job of camouflaging the blitz than ever before, there are still too many ways to spot it, to anticipate it. The linebackers will cheat up to the line before the ball is snapped, whereas usually they're two or three yards back. It doesn't do a linebacker any good to blitz from three yards back, so when you see him fudging up toward the line, you've got to smell a blitz.

You can also watch the free safety for information on a blitzing probability. Normally the free safety has no specific responsibility and he plays pretty deep. But if there's a weak side blitz coming up, the free safety has a definite responsibility: He has to cover the first back out of the backfield, and in order to get into position to do this, he can't be his usual 12 or 15 yards from the line of scrimmage, he's got to cheat up so he's only seven or eight yards away. So you've got to get suspicious. Similarly, when the two outside linebackers are going to blitz, the middle linebacker will often give it away. Instead of his usual job, he has to cover the first back out of the backfield on the strong side. Whenever I see him edging over toward the strong side to get head up with the offensive back on that side, I've got to say to myself, "Well, old Moe there must be expecting the two outside linebackers to blitz." None of this sounds too complicated when you put it down on paper, but I've covered only a small fraction of the ways in which blitzes can be tipped off, and you've got to go up to the line and figure all this out practically instantly. More and more offenses are able to do this and they are making the blitz too big a gamble to last much longer.

The blitz reached its peak a few years ago. It was the big weapon against the pass, but now it is being superseded by a far more effective weapon, the pass rush. I wince when I think of the pass rush that's being put on by some of the teams in pro ball these days. Just for an idea, look at the Detroit Lions' pass rush. Your best rushers are usually ends. They come crashing in on you from the outside the way Andy Robustelli used to, but against Detroit you not only have the ends but you have two All-Pro tackles, Alex Karras and Roger Brown, slamming right up the middle. You just can't ask your guards to hold that 300-pound Brown and that big bull Karras for very long, and you have to make adjustments against the Lions like setting your pocket deeper.

Back when I broke into pro football, you had a

few good pass rushers, guys like Robustelli, Gino Marchetti, Jim Katcavage, and one or two others. But now you've got 20 or 25 super pass rushers around the league, and every team has a few guys who'll be beating on you all afternoon. To my mind, these pass rushers are unique in sport. You can't show me another sport that asks a man to be not big but *huge,* preferably 260 pounds and up, preferably at least 6′ 5″, and still be as quick as a sprinter off the blocks and plenty nimble on his feet. The pass rusher has got to be a combination of professional wrestler, Olympic 100-meter man, and ballet dancer. At Minnesota, two of the five fastest men on our squad were defensive pass rushers: Carl Eller and Jim Marshall. They tell me that the fastest man on the Los Angeles team when they timed them several years ago was David Jones, the pass rusher, and he's 6′ 5″ and 270 pounds. Merlin Olsen was hardly a step behind him. Henry Jordan and Willie Davis, of the Packers, have great speed. So do Bob Lilly of the Cowboys, Ordell Braase of the Colts, and Doug Atkins of the Bears, and they're all behemoths.

Pass rushers are the *dramatis personae* in my nightmares. Some of them have been notoriously effective against me (Willie Davis of the Packers, to name one), and I'll spend half the afternoon with them draped all over me, banging me down and sitting on me. A lot of people have asked me

106

how I managed to hold my temper when I saw the 245 pounds of Willie Davis flying through the air at me for the fourth time in a game, how I kept from calling him some kind of insulting name or pulling his nose, or doing something nasty? Well, that's one of the first things you learn as a professional quarterback: *Do not alienate the pass rushers.* Guys like Willie Davis are tough enough when they're in a good mood. If you go out of your way to get them mad, you're asking for more trouble than I personally wish to encounter at eye level. And I also don't want them to know that they're bothering me in the least, I don't want them to think that they're disturbing my afternoon one bit. So when they knock me down, I usually say something like, "Good play, nice going!" I'll say, "Deacon, you're really getting in on me today!" Or "Ordell, is it you again?" I'll say, "My gosh, Willie, you're spending the whole afternoon in my backfield!" Or "Listen, Roger, why don't you get in my huddle? You've been back here all day anyway." My slogan is: Always leave 'em smiling. That way you hold their adrenalin flow down a little.

And, in the second place, a quarterback is a football player just like everybody else out there and he's *supposed* to get hit. The pass rusher is *supposed* to get him. The pass rusher is not out there to deliver a spray of forget-me-nots. He's supposed to bang you as hard as he can, knock your teeth out, bruise you all over your body, break you up and shake you up. I try not to let it bother me. I've got my own work to do. Do you realize that when you're lying on the ground with 600 pounds of pass rushers on top of you, it's kind of peaceful down there? It's a good time to be planning your next play (or your retirement!). There isn't a quarterback in pro football who doesn't put the pleasant interlude to good use.

I'm not primarily a runner, except in emergencies, and maybe I'd take an entirely different approach if I were. A runner like Jim Taylor hated to get tackled, and sometimes after a play you'd see him standing there jawing at the guy who had stopped him. Jim Taylor never handed out any compliments or wisecracks when he got tackled! He ran force against force, twisting, squirming, and struggling. The other guy would struggle back, and it became a personal kind of thing. Taylor would get up from a tackle fighting mad, because he was so competitive that he didn't think he should ever be tackled. He regarded it as a personal affront. He harnessed his anger and his temper — one reason why he was such a fine runner. A quarterback is different, he's got to be a little cooler. As a rule, I just sort of go *thunk* when I'm tackled, like a sack of meal, because my mind isn't on moving forward but on completing a pass, hitting a target. I've got a million things to think about, and getting knocked on my back is one of the last.

Sometimes it seems there's no end to the miniscule details you have to remember on a pro football field, right down to the way you tie your shoes, and the reason is that the teams in the pro game are so evenly matched that the little things often decide games. The No. 1 bromide about pro ball has always been: "On any given Sunday, any team in the NFL can beat any other." Right. And if the teams are just about equal in major matters, you'd better get your minor matters down pat. In the case of a quarterback, that even includes how he uses his mouth, his larynx, his vocal chords. The way you count cadence can cost you a game, and the way you call a play in the huddle can make or break your offense. You've got to exude confidence. It can't be faked. You've got to know your job backwards. You've got to sound self-assured and *be* self-assured. When you lean over that center and start your cadence count, you can't do it in a cracking, timid voice. You can't stumble around. It's a funny thing, but they tell me that Bart Starr used to be that way when he first came up but, as you may have noticed, he licked the problem pretty fast. The simple truth is the good quarterback has to be a loudmouth. He has to be heard all the way from the flanker back on the left to the split end on the right, and that's a distance of 25 or 30 yards.

In the huddle, the quarterback has to be equally sure of himself. If you go into the huddle and stumble around and change your play two or three times, your teammates will quickly realize that you don't know what you're doing. If I go into the huddle and say, "Open four right 29 . . . no, no, no, 25 I trap . . . no, that's no good, let's run something else, a 48 zip," I've lost my own teammates. They figure this guy doesn't have the slightest idea what the situation calls for. How can we follow a leader like that? All quarterbacks stumble around once in a while, but if it becomes a habit, forget it!

A quarterback also has to watch his diction, and if you think that sounds silly, consider the fact that only one of the other 10 men has to misunderstand a signal and the whole play can be shot: More than likely, it *will* be shot. You can't go into the huddle sounding like Gomer Pyle or Lady Bird Johnson. You've got to say, "Open four right 29 G O on two" in pear-shaped tones, with total clarity, not "Open foe rat twinny nan G O own tew." That's how a lot of plays are busted. There's no room for the least misunderstanding.

I remember one day when we were doing a skeleton pass drill at Minnesota and Lee Grosscup, The Cupper, one of the really funny men of the era, was quarterbacking. Now "The Cupper" was an American original, he never liked to do things in the old, tired style. So he was calling a play real loud in the huddle, and he chose his own way of saying that the play would be run on the count of two. The Cupper said, "All right, we'll run this on the deuce. *On the deuce!*"

Van Brocklin was standing 50 yards away and he covered the distance in about five seconds flat. He said, "Grosscup, we don't want any of that Madison Avenue fertilizer around here! When you mean two, say two, not the deuce!" We all got a big laugh out of it later, but Van Brocklin was absolutely right. Nothing less than 100 per cent simplicity will do in a pro football huddle. A quarterback has to practice Allie Sherman's "KISS" system! "Keep It Simple, Stupid!"

And even after the poor old quarterback has followed these rules, kept his language simple and forceful, learned the opposition defense and how to probe it, done his homework and studied his scouting reports, been a good boy and helped old ladies across the street, he still might lose the ball game. Maybe the other team's quarterback has been a good boy, too, or maybe the other team has just too many guns. Or maybe the other team benefits from that vastly underrated phenomenon of pro football: The factor of luck, fate, the breaks, call it what you will. I've never heard two or more pro quarterbacks get together without going into a long discussion of the breaks and how you can do everything right and still lose the game on one lousy, rotten, unfair, and unexpected break of the game. To my mind there's no doubt about it. Luck enters into everything, and more than averagely into pro football. And since pro football is a game of momentum, you can lose a ball game by 35-0 because of one little break that goes against you early in the game. You *shouldn't,* but you can.

I don't have much patience with these people who say that the breaks all even up over the long pull. You're not playing over the long pull, you're playing right now, and it tears you apart to lose on a dirty bounce, a missed call, or some kind of lucky break. I remember a time in 1965, when we needed one touchdown in the last two minutes to beat Green Bay. Well, we scored *two.* The first was called back for offensive pass interference and the second because an official said the receiver was out-of-bounds. And the game film showed that both calls were questionable. That was good luck on the part of the Packers, but you couldn't have found that out from the standings. And if the Packers hadn't won that game, they couldn't have won the Western Division championship, and they would never have gotten a chance to beat Cleveland for the league championship. So don't anybody tell me that luck doesn't play a big part. I'm not sour-graping about it, I'm simply stating facts that are well-known to NFL players.

In that same season, Green Bay tied Baltimore in the last period of the playoff game, then went on to beat the Colts in overtime and win the Western Division championship. After the game was over, everybody rushed to see the game film and it looked to many as though the field goal that had tied the game was wide. Baltimore lost the game on a break, on a matter of centimeters.

Or just take the subject of fumbles. Once a ball is fumbled, everything that happens after that is 90 per cent luck. The ball squirts this way and that and somebody winds up jumping on it, and he's either a friend or foe, depending on how the breaks are going that day. In the NFL championship game in 1966, Mel Renfro came out of the end zone for Dallas and fumbled the ball on his own 18, and a Packer back — Jim Grabowski — picked it up and ran for a touchdown. This was luck, the breaks. How many times is Renfro going to fumble like that? How many times is a running back going to be standing right there when the ball gets loose? How many times is he going to have total daylight in front of him?

Later in the same game, Dallas went in for the tying touchdown and the left tackle was offside. Sure, the left tackle made a bad play, but how about the other 10 guys on the Dallas offensive team? Were they victimized by their bad team play? No, by a break of the game. Suppose the tackle had been offside on the previous play or the next play instead of the key one that ties the game? These are breaks, and breaks play a big part in the game of football, a far bigger part than most members of the establishment are willing to admit.

I know there's an old trite saying that the best disciplined team makes its own breaks, makes its own luck, and this is true. But there are lots of breaks that nobody can understand, breaks that have nothing whatever to do with a team's discipline or skill. How about the situation where you throw a pass at one of your receivers and suddenly you see that the ball is headed right into the arms of a cornerback, and then out of nowhere comes another one of your receivers to pick off the ball on the dead run? The rookie quarterback will say to himself, "Boy, I am some passer." The veteran will say, "How lucky can I get?" Believe me, it is possible to get *plenty* lucky in the NFL. It is possible to slop into a victory. The win is usually to the better team, but not always.

# 5

When one of his teammates would blow a play, quarterback Bobby Layne used to call him everything under the sun, kick him in the tail, and question his ancestry in a voice you could hear all the way to Youngstown, Ohio. Five minutes after the outburst, Bobby and the victim of his wrath would walk off the field with their arms around each other. Everybody on the team knew that Bobby didn't mean anything he said when the heat was on. It was just his way of riling up the ball club.

Norm Van Brocklin was another one like that. He ran his offense the way a South African diamond mine foreman runs his diggers. He used everything out there except a whip, and he'd have

115

used that if the league would have granted permission. When you played alongside Van Brocklin, you expected to get chewed out three or four times a game. That was just his style, and you adapted to it or you sought other employment.

I cite Layne and Van Brocklin as two of the more extreme examples of the tough quarterback, but when they played that was more or less the style. And they had great success with it. Maybe the average pro football player was a different type of person in those days. I don't know, I wasn't there. But personally I can't play quarterback in the old hellfire-and-brimstone way. I can't hold a whip over a teammate. It's just not my style. And I think you'll find it's not the style of many other pro quarterbacks nowadays.

I don't mean to say that I never snap at my teammates, but I do mean to say that I do it rarely. When I beef at somebody, it's either because I can't think of any other way of getting the most out of him, or it's because I've just plain let the tension get to me, in which case I'll go out of my way to right the wrong in any way I can. I think this is true of most of the other pro quarterbacks, too. A guy like Bart Starr, the prototype of the polite, reserved, considerate quarterback, doesn't throw temper tantrums. Once, during the heat of action, Bart smacked his great guard Jerry Kramer in the tail and said, "C'mon, Jerry, let's go!" And the next day Bart took Jerry aside and apologized.

That's old Bart. He's just a great old fellow, a real fine person. He gains the respect of his teammates by performance, on and off the field, not by calling them all a bunch of meatheads everytime they make a mistake. You can't do that any more in the world of business, and you can't do it anymore in the world of football. You're dealing with an entirely different breed of cat out there from the players of the past, and the quarterback who lets his inner sadistic impulses bubble up to the top soon finds himself on the road with a complete sample kit, ringing doorbells and wondering where he went wrong.

Of course, there will always be players who have to be coerced, who practically beg you to ride them, and there still are a few who are remnants of the past, guys you won't budge unless you get on them a little. They are growing rare, but you still have to deal with one or two. That was one of the raps on me when I first came to the game, that I was too nice and that I wouldn't be able to handle the ball players who had to be pushed. The nicely-nicely stuff grew out of the fact that I was a quiet kid from the South, a Joe College, a preacher's son, and all that. Anybody with that kind of background had to be too soft and subdued to make it as a pro quarterback. Well, luckily I'm not too nice for the National Football League. I can scream and holler with the best of them, but I'm always ashamed of myself when I do it without a very good reason. And whatever I say to a man, I try not to degrade him. I know there are some coaches and a few quarterbacks who on rare occasions will degrade a player, but I will not do it, nor will *I* be degraded, and if you took a poll around the league, you would find that the other players feel the same way.

Sometimes it's tough to hold your tongue, and sometimes it's impossible. I think the maddest I ever got was a long time ago when I called a pass pattern to the left at a crucial moment in a big game. If that pattern didn't develop, then I was going to try to hit my flankerback on the right, who was supposed to be running a deep drag-in pattern. I dropped back, set up in the pocket, looked for my primary receiver on the left and found him surrounded by the wrong color shirts. I turned quickly to my alternative receiver on the right and that character was barely in motion. He hadn't even made his turn to come down the middle and, at the rate he was trotting, he would be in position to take my pass about next Tuesday. Boy, I flamed! There was absolutely nothing to do now but run for my life, and I did.

After the play was over, I ran to Van Brocklin as fast as my stubby little legs could carry me. "Get that guy out of there!" I said. "This is the big play of the game and he's supposed to be giving 500 per cent and he's out there picking flowers!" That's the only time in my career that

118

I ever threw anybody out of a game, and I tried not to turn it into a public matter, but I just wasn't going to play with a guy who would let a team down like that.

There have been other times when I've said things I regretted, and I'd just have to hope that my teammates understood that the tension got to me and I didn't mean it. I once threw a pass to Bill Brown, one of my best friends in the world, and Boom Boom couldn't quite get to it, probably because it was thrown long, but I was really upset. It was a third-down play, and when Bill came to the sidelines, I yelled at him, "Boom Boom, you gotta stretch out for it!" Right away I felt like stitching up my mouth. If there's a guy in the league who puts out on every play, it's Bill Brown, and I spent the rest of the afternoon patting him on the back for just about everything he did. I think he understood.

A few years before, when we had a tough little guard named Gerry Huth, I dropped back into the pocket and a pass rusher came out of nowhere and knocked me flat. I kept quiet, but when the same thing happened on the next play, I got up and hollered, "Gerry, you've got to block that guy! You can't let him keep coming in on me all day long! I can't throw when your man's all over me!" *And it wasn't even Gerry's man.* After the game, I said, "Hootie, I'm sorry. I really goofed." And I learned a lesson.

Sometimes it works the other way around: Sometimes somebody will get on me, and then it's my turn to be patient and understanding. We were playing Green Bay in 1964 and it was third down and short yardage. And I didn't know then what I know now about the Packers, so I went for the long bomb and it was knocked down. Coming off the field a guard named Palmer Pyle, a real veteran, hollered at me, "Why the hell don't we go and get the first down?"

I understood that Palmer was all tied up in the game, that he didn't really mean to be so loudly critical, but on the other hand I had to keep control of the team, so I snapped right back. "Listen," I said. "I'll run this game and I'll call the plays and you just play your position and shut up!" He was a nice guy, and he didn't mean anything by his remark, but I had to let him know it was my show out there. It's very important for teammates to show the greatest confidence in each other. If I start getting on guys for missing blocks, what are they supposed to think if I throw four straight incompletions? Should they start telling me I'm lousy, that I should shape up out there? A lot of the time it's my own fault. I'm holding the ball too long, or I'm calling the wrong plays, or I'm misreading the defense. But if I miss four straight, should my teammates get mad at me? Why, heck, no. We're on a team, and we're after the same objective, and if I miss four straight, they've got to believe that I'll connect on the next 20! And if one of my linemen misses his block four straight times, I've got to believe that he'll make that block every time for the rest of the game.

Personally, I think a quarterback should go out of his way to use positive criticism, to compliment and praise whenever it's due and try to keep his mouth shut when it's not. When I praise somebody on our ball club, I really mean it. A lineman who knocks a blitzer on his back, or a flanker who goes 30 yards down the field and then makes a perfect fake and cuts the other way so I can hit him with a pass — why, those guys have done beautiful things. Just doing *average* things in the pro game takes a tremendous effort. It's not the kind of job where you can roll along on 90 per cent of your potential. Everybody in the pro game is a great athlete in my book. The rawest rookie in the NFL deserves my respect because he's already beaten out — how many? — more than 600 college players to get where he is. He is a dedicated, disciplined, conditioned competitor, and he doesn't deserve to have his nose rubbed in the dirt whenever he makes a mistake.

I don't know, maybe I'm a little overprejudiced in favor of the contemporary pro football player. I think we've got the highest type of person, among the brightest and best men that our society can produce. Look at some of them. Bill Glass is a minister. Bill McColl and Dave Middleton are both medical doctors. Yale Lary was elected to the Texas Legislature while he was still in the league. The modern pro player may be a real estate magnate like Larry Morris, he may be a movie actor like Jimmy Brown, or a chain restaurateur like Gino Marchetti. He's a sophisticated professional, he's educated, he travels in cultured circles, he hobnobs with top business men, traveling and learning. He plays an important role in his community. He realizes that he has to close the gap between his potential and his achievement. In the off-time, you'll find pro football players speaking to young people's groups all over the country. Raymond Berry, Prentice Gautt, Bob Vogel, Bart Starr, Curtis McClinton, Bill Curry, and Maxie Baughan are just a few who do. They realize that they are idolized and watched constantly by young kids, and they try to be worthy.

I don't know how to pinpoint the exact time when the pro football standards jumped way up, but almost overnight the game seemed to reach the point where you just couldn't afford unintelligent players. Suddenly you had to draw pass patterns with a whole picture involved and everybody on the team had to understand the possibilities and go out there with two or three options in mind. An offensive lineman who used to have the job of knocking one specific opponent on his backside suddenly had to learn a special kind of blocking, because the defenses started stunting all over the place. The defender would line up across from the offensive lineman. But on the snap of the ball, everything would change. Instead of coming right over the offensive lineman, the defender would slant through another hole and another defender would pop up in his place. And while the poor offensive linemen was trying to catch up with his man, another defensive lineman was going right through the vacated hole.

This kind of stunting brought "area blocking" into football, sort of a zone defense in blocking, and it put plenty of mental pressure on every offensive lineman. He might be lined up head to head with the right tackle, but the right tackle might make his charge over the center, with the linebacker right behind him, and the offensive lineman had to know how to react instantly. Sam Huff and Joe Schmidt and guys like that helped to cause a lot of this change. They'd roam free behind the line and pop through the holes opened by head-to-head blocking. The instant that area blocking became the norm, the immobile, slow-thinking offensive lineman was dead and buried.

For my money, the offensive lineman who evolved out of that period of change is probably the most underrated player in the game. Fans know less about offensive linemen than anybody else on the team including the kicker. Offensive linemen are the forgotten players. They never make a tackle, they never touch the ball, they never make a touchdown or intercept a pass. For the most part they have very little freedom of movement — they have to stay in a disciplined position; make their blocks and try to catch their breath for the next play while the backs and the ends are strutting around like heroes. When the offensive lineman does his job, he's practically invisible, and when he doesn't, everybody within four miles can see him flub the block. I tell you, that offensive lineman has the toughest job in pro football. The defensive lineman has to learn three or four basic charges and that's it, but the offensive lineman has to have exactly the same knowledge of plays that a back has, and he's got to learn to react to the charge of the defense and adjust his blocking instantly and execute without error. *And he's getting hit on every play!* Those pulverizing pass rushers are all over him; he's in the game for 60 plays and he gets hit on every one.

You have to wonder what makes a guy like that play the game, and, for that matter, what makes the pro football player take the punishment, self-inflicted and otherwise, that is a part of pro ball. Right away you're going to say: It's the money. Well, very few of us could afford to play football for love. But I can tell you that the money is secondary, that the money matters very little in the final analysis. Last season you kept hearing how the Colts and the Jets were going to play for big money in the Super Bowl, and how that would make them really put out. Anybody who believed that doesn't know the Colts and the Jets. Money is nice, money is great, but money doesn't motivate. Winning for winning's sake is the motivation, not dollars. No, I've never given back any of the money that I've earned playing football, and I get in there and bargain my head off when it's salary time, but once that's all behind me I'm playing to win, I'm out there to win, and winning is all that's on my mind. If Pete Rozelle had announced just before the Super Bowl game that the entire receipts were going to charity, the game would have been played exactly as it was, right down to the last extra point. Those guys would have paid to play each other!

There isn't a man alive who would take the pounding, the discipline, the personal hell that the pro player has to go through, solely for money. And yet college coaches will send one of their players around and they'll say, "Old Joe here has all the tools, but he never really played well for me. But boy, when you put that money on the line, he'll be terrific!" Old Joe never makes it. Money simply doesn't motivate. Look at Arnold Palmer, beating his brains out on the pro tour. Does anybody think he's doing it for the money alone? Why, Arnold Palmer has to hire men to count the men who count his money! He's out there for the challenge and the inspiration of winning. With all his money, Arnold Palmer is still hungry. He's hungry to achieve. People like to say so-and-so is a hungry athlete, and they think that means he's hungry for money. That's not what a hungry athlete is at all. A hungry athlete is a guy who hasn't won as much as he should have won, or as much as his pride makes him think he should have won. A prime example comes to mind: Me, I'm a hungry quarterback. I reckon I'm about the hungriest quarterback in the National Football League. In eight years, I haven't won a championship, and man, I'm starved! But not for money. For winning, for satisfying myself, for reaching my goals.

You've got to be hungry and you've got to want to win, and you've got to love the game of football to stand up under the pressures of the pro game. The average college hotshot has no idea what the pro pressure is like. It's the difference between building model airplanes and piloting a 707, and it's a terrible transition to make. In college you get a four-year scholarship and it doesn't matter whether you play fifth-string or first-string, you've still got it made. This is the fallacy in the college scholarship system. You can go there and sit on your tail for four years and do nothing while the other guys are breaking themselves in half on the football field earning your keep for you. But in pro football there's no such thing. There are 100 other boys lurking around the coach's office looking for your job, and then you go out on Sunday and you have maybe 30 minutes of playing time to show that you are the right person for the job. Man that's pressure!

Some mighty fine people don't even make it to the game-playing stage of pro football. They break right down in training camp. I remember one great-looking college kid who came to the Vikings a little overweight after his senior year of school, and he groaned and moaned as though he was dying out there at camp. He'd say to me, "Oh, this is just too much for me. I can't make it; I'll have to quit." Tommy Mason and I sat him down and told him he'd have to take everything that was dished out in training camp or go home right now, and that kid went out there and really pushed, really made an effort. He was cut on the next-to-last day of practice.

Coaches are constantly watching to see if anybody goofs off the least little bit in training camp, because the guy who doesn't put out in training camp is the guy who's going to quit on you with third-and-one in the last quarter. We used to keep tabs on the shortest training careers in Vikings' history. For a long time the record holder was a big old tackle who came into camp weighing over 300 pounds and right away was sent out to do some zig-zag running through the ropes. The ropes are stretched out in a grid about a foot above the ground and you have to run through those squares with your knees pumping good and high, twisting and juking the whole time. Well, this big old boy went through the ropes one-and-a-half times and then fell down on the ground. He was twitching around there and pretty soon we could hear him say, "Send me to the church! Where's the church? Take me to the church!" He thought he was dying. When he snapped out of it, Van Brocklin cut him on the spot. Anybody who couldn't go through the ropes more than once would never make it as a pro.

That tackle lasted maybe a half hour, but records are made to be broken. Here comes a castoff fullback from another NFL team, and he pulls into our training camp just as we're doing calisthenics which, as everybody knows, is more fun than a barrel of rattlesnakes, but not much more. So on the first exercise the old gentleman announces that he can't do this one; he's got a bad leg. On the second exercise, he says he can't do this one either; an old hip operation is hurting. Van Brocklin walked over and said, "You've had it! Pack your bags!" So far as I know, that record still stands. Ten minutes.

I doubt if the average person has the slightest conception of the pure pain a pro football player has to take just to make the team, and on top of that there's the pure pain that may hit him after the kick-off. People say to me, "Aren't you scared of getting hurt out there?" And the answer is no. I recognize the dangers of pro football, but I've also learned the disciplines of the game, just like every other NFL player. Before I went up to the pros, I used to wonder: How can those pro quarterbacks stand it, with guys like Marchetti and Big Daddy Lipscomb booming in on them? How in the world can they take a beating like that? But I found out that once you're involved in the game you forget about physical contact. I hardly even feel it when I'm hit. I have to take an awful shot before the pain reaches me. You can say: "No sense, no feeling," but that's not it. The thing is, you get so highly involved that your brain simply doesn't react to pain or fear in a normal way. *There's no time.*

Of course, there are bound to be times when players do get hurt and do feel pain. But more often than not, they'll keep right on playing. It isn't that they're so courageous either, it's that they have disciplined themselves to the point where they instinctively do things like putting their heads down and ramming other people in the stomach. It hurts, sure it does, but discipline has taught them how to endure the pain and make the tackle or throw the block. Fear and hurt become recessive; making the play is all that matters. You can't be a polished football player as long as you're thinking about the hurt and the pain and the fear. Sometimes I think that of all the qualities that go to make up a pro football player, the most underestimated one is that capacity to take punishment and not let it detract one tiny bit from your performance. Usually the team that's willing to hurt the most is the team that wins the most. And this is something you only learn as you play. Your threshold of pain gets higher and higher. The pros play with separated shoulders, twisted knees, sprained ankles, and bruised ribs. The philosophy is that if they've got 14 games to go and they can walk out on that field, they can play.

Nobody comes into the pro league with this ability built in. During my last season with the Vikings, we had a big rookie tackle named Doug Davis, a really fine ball player. Just before we were going to play Baltimore, he suffered a shoulder injury. Doug was very important to our game plan and we needed him. Well, on one of the first offensive plays he got hit right in that sore shoulder and you could see in his eyes the agony he was going through. He staggered over to me and without opening his mouth he made it plain that he had to get off that playing field. I said, "Rookie, get your head up! You're not hurt! Get in the huddle!" I had to convince him that he wasn't hurt as bad as he was, make him not think

130

about it and play the game. I wanted him mad at me, because that would help him forget the pain. I love old Doug, but it had to be done that way, and he played the rest of the game and played well.

The courage of some of the older pros never fails to amaze me — it's fantastic and it's inspiring. I watched David Parks of the San Francisco 49ers playing against us with a set of the most bruised and battered ribs you could imagine. Now you can play a whole ball game with a bad arm or a bad thigh or something like that and never get hurt, if you're lucky, but with bruised ribs you've got to get hurt on just about every play. In this game, the 49ers sent Dave Parks out on the field encased in tape from neck to waist. He would line up kind of stiffly, but on the snap he'd leave that line of scrimmage full-blast, tear down there, catch that pass, and then get thrown to the ground in a pile of knuckles and elbows. He'd haul himself off the field, let the pain ease a little, and go right out and do it again. Once he got hit with a forearm in the sore ribs when he was down along the sidelines — one of those things that happen in the heat of play — and two plays later he was back on the field catching another pass and going through the torture all over again. And remember: This was late in the season, and the 49ers weren't going any place,

there was nothing much at stake, *except to win.*
And Dave Parks went out there to win, that's
just the way Dave Parks is. The 49ers lost the
game 28-3, and Dave never scored a touchdown,
but he should have got the game ball six times
over.

I've seen plenty of pro players put on the same
kind of exhibition. I've seen Johnny Unitas barely
able to wobble off the field after a tackle and
then on the next series of offensive downs, he
would be right back in there throwing. I've seen
the time when he had to be helped off the field by
his teammates, he was hurting so bad. And I've
watched another Baltimore player, Raymond Berry, come back and play after a knee operation,
limping down the field on his pass pattern three
weeks after the knee had been laid wide open in
the operating room.

There are some pro fans who think that we go
out there on the football field and try to mutilate
each other. Let me tell you: That idea is exactly
100 per cent wrong. I am absolutely certain that
there is not a player in the NFL who consciously
tries to knock another player out of a game. Sure,
we hit as hard as we can, but that's what we're
supposed to do. Football is a contact spot, a
Spartan game. But there's a big difference between
hitting somebody because that's part of the game,
and hitting somebody with the intention of in-

juring him. And yet a lot of people think that teams make mass efforts to injure certain key players on the opposition. I've heard it said that when you're injured, you can't rub the hurt because if the other team finds out where it is, then everybody will be shooting for that sore spot to get you out of the game. People must think we're boxers, working on each other's sore noses! When you start aiming for a certain spot on an opposition ball player, you're forgetting 16 other things you're supposed to be doing yourself, and that's a whole lot more important than sending somebody to the sidelines with an injury.

The truth is, there's much less dirty football than people think, but if it helps attendance for them to think that we're all out there trying to maim one another, then let them think it. Of course, there's a very short distance between aggressive football and dirty football, and frequently one appears indistinguishable from the other, especially when you're sitting in row 74. An aggressive player is going to hit after the whistle now and then because he's going so hard that his momentum can't be stopped. We had a lot of that at Minnesota. We were a very aggressive football team, we *had* to be. But it doesn't follow that we were a dirty football team, even though you will still hear that said around the league. People used to come to me and ask, "How can a preacher's son like you condone the way your ball club plays so dirty?" And I'd try to explain that we weren't dirty, we were aggressive. A new-franchise team doesn't have the personnel, it doesn't have a lot of ability, but it can make up for a lot of its deficiencies by playing hard. Our team hit anything that moved! And we got a lot of criticism for it.

In the Green Bay-Minnesota games during my last two or three years with the Vikings, the Packers suffered from serious injuries. Maybe that's because we played extra hard against the Packers, I don't know. I do know it isn't because we played dirty against them, although that complaint was made publicly. Extra-hard is the way the game is *supposed* to be played. Personally, I think what bothered the Green Bay fans was that they were supposed to beat us big, and they never did. If you looked at the personnel of the two teams, the Packers should have destroyed us. And when they didn't, why, we had to be hatchet men!

Well, I can't deny that Paul Hornung hurt his knee against us. He came running into the line and one of our players ducked his head and got Paul right in the knee with his helmet. These things happen. I hope there's nobody up around Green Bay who seriously thinks that our player carefully timed the exact instant when he could hit Paul in the knee with his head! And I also hope that there's nobody in Green Bay who thinks that we carefully picked the precise way to hit their fine guard, Jerry Kramer, so that we could break his leg. Years ago things like that were done intentionally. Teams used to have hatchet men, enforcers, just like certain defensemen on pro hockey teams. But pro football players can't afford to be that naïve anymore. There are too many perceptions and realizations and classifications to order in your minds, too many split-second decisions to make with accuracy. You just don't have time to go out there and pretend you're the Green Hornet.

# 6

Shortly after I was traded from the Vikings to the Giants on March 8, 1967, some people began saying, "So, that's the reason he quit in Minnesota, he wanted to play in New York." Actually, I didn't have any choice about where I was going to be playing. The Vikings were simply going to trade me to whatever team would give them the most in return. I came close to playing for several other clubs — the Chicago Bears, the Detroit Lions, or the Pittsburgh Steelers. Those three teams made strong bids for my services, and, as I understand it, I very nearly went to the Bears.

All things considered, a football player would like to play in New York sometime in his life because of the exposure he can get there and because it will enhance his career after his playing days have ended. All you have to do is to look at Kyle Rote, Pat Summerall, Frank Gifford, and others to realize the value of playing for a New York team. It can mean a great deal when you have peeled off your uniform for the last time and start to look for work elsewhere.

How knowledgeable the New York fans are is hard for me to know. They are probably as well read on pro football as any group of fans anywhere. Reading newspapers and magazines, though, does not necessarily mean that they — or the fans in any other city — are truly knowledgeable. I say this because I know football is a difficult sport to cover. I am sure that if I were a writer covering pro football I would have as hard a time as he does. Sportswriters know that they can't go around all year writing nothing but words of glowing praise about their teams. Such pablum would cost them readers. Since both the writers and the readers know that every team has faults, it is understandable that these shortcomings should be examined in print. I don't object to this, for the only ones worse at judging talent are the players and coaches themselves. What I do object to is that so much of what is written is inaccurate, some of it outrageously so. I am amazed sometimes that so many errors, both in fact and analysis, appear in print.

When I signed my contract for the 1968 season

the stories carried in the New York newspapers were so dissimilar that it was hard to believe they were all reporting about the same player. All attributed their inside information to "knowledgeable sources." That implied that those writers knew what they were writing about. Yet one reported that my contract called for a salary of $40,000, another said I had signed a three-year package for $200,000, and a third paper was somewhere in between. The only thing that was right in any of the stories was that I had signed for one year. As far as the salary, nobody, despite what their "knowledgeable sources" said, was even in the ball park.

One way to get some idea of how hard it is to cover pro football is to look at the All-Pro teams. I couldn't even begin to list the players I felt deserved to be on the defensive line. As closely as I watch the game and as often as I look at game films, I still find it almost impossible to be overly aware of who's doing what on the offensive line. The writers who vote for the All-Pro team are just as hard put as the rest of us when it comes to singling out the best offensive linemen and when they are filling out their ballots they do what anybody else would do: They put down the names of players they have read the most about.

Take the case of Mick Tingelhoff, a center. Mick was named center on the All-Pro team five years ago, after Jim Ringo had won it for eons. I told Mick, "You've got the title from now until you retire." It has turned out to be absolutely true. He *may* be the best center there is. I must admit, though, that I don't know if he is or not. The point is, he no longer *has* to be the best because his reputation has been established and those who do the balloting know his name.

Because I feel so strongly about the inaccuracies in the sports pages, I *never* read a word they have to say about the Giants from the time I go to training camp until the season has ended. I do this because I think it can be dangerous if a player starts believing what he reads about his teammates. Players may realize that what they are reading is hogwash but, even so, some of that stuff becomes engrained in their minds. Suppose I read in somebody's column that Homer Jones can't go to his right. I *know* that Homer Jones can go to his right, but if I start reading that he can't I'm liable to start asking myself, "I wonder if Homer Jones *can* go to his right?" This creates doubts and that can only lead to trouble. I don't want my opinion of my teammates to be altered because of something I read by a reporter who can't possibly know my teammates as well as I do. Oh, I'll read about opposing teams, but I hold fast to my ban on reading about my own until the season is over. It takes discipline not to read about your team or yourself and I have to skip here and there around the sports pages to avoid doing so.

I don't expect other players to adhere to this sort of thing, but for me it's a strict rule.

Now that I am a Giant, I feel that New York is the best place in the world to play football. I think that the people of New York appreciate pro football more than the fans of any city I have been to. They can be caressing and loving, and they can be vicious and aggravating. But, above all, they let you know that they care. Sometimes they boo. They have booed me and there have been times when I have played so poorly that I wanted to stand right in the middle of the field and boo myself.

Fans relate the failure of their team to the quarterback more than to any other player. When a team is winning it means that all parts are functioning well and when this is the case it is easy for the fans to cheer anyone and everyone. When a team is losing it is natural that the quarterback should take the brunt of the abuse from the fans. Those people in the stands can't be expected to dissect the play of the offensive line, the defensive, and the horde of other players on the field. After all, the players and writers can't do this either, so how can we expect the fans to be aware of all the little things that are going on down on the field? But when a team is not playing well it is easy to pick out the quarterback's mistakes. Ergo, it is the quarterback whose ears are given a blistering.

Surprisingly, many coaches react the same way the fans do, laying the blame for all defeats on the quarterback. Some coaches have simply placed too high a value on the quarterback. They feel that if they can come up with a good quarterback it will somehow make up for shortcomings in the team's defensive secondary or that it will somehow help the team's punting, field goal kicking, and offensive line play. You'll find coaches who time and again will bring in some youngster who has never been tried before and announce that he's going to be the one to lead the club out of the wilderness. And the poor young quarterback is going to be worse off than ever because as long as the rest of the team has weaknesses he can only accomplish so much and no more. You'd think this wouldn't happen in pro football, but it does.

Another mistake made by some coaches is that they label quarterbacks as those who can't win a championship and those who can. That's a bunch of malarky. Winning a championship depends not so much on how good your quarterback is as it does on how good the rest of the team is. There has been no better example of this than the Baltimore Colts of recent years. When Johnny Unitas was hurt in 1965 it looked like the end for the Colts. But Gary Cuozzo took over and became a tremendous quarterback. Then Cuozzo was injured and it really looked like the end for the Colts. How could they possibly win without a quarterback? Well, they did. Halfback Tom Matte became the quarterback and he beat the Rams and nearly upset the Packers in the playoff game.

In 1968 Unitas was ailing again and the Colts had to get another passer. They tried to get Jim Ninowski. They couldn't get him, so they settled for Earl Morrall, who's a perfect example of what I am driving at. During his first dozen years in the NFL he played on four different teams, didn't gain much attention, and was labled as the type of quarterback who couldn't win a championship. And what was accomplished in 1968 by Morrall, the man four other teams had given up on and the quarterback the Colts didn't really want? All he did was lead the Colts to their best season ever and to the championship of the NFL. This proves to me that labeling quarterbacks is unfair. Morrall didn't become a superior quarterback overnight. He was the same competent Earl Morrall he has always been, but in 1968 he was blessed with a supporting cast that was better than any he had ever had.

Take the case of Bart Starr. As long as Green Bay had Paul Hornung and Jim Taylor and then was able to replace them with runners like Elijah Pitts, Donny Anderson, Jim Grabowski, and Travis Williams, the Packers were virtually unbeatable. And as long as the Packers were able to keep their runners and almost everyone else on the team healthy, they kept on winning. Through it all, Bart

Starr was classified as a winner. Then came 1968. Injuries beset Starr and a multitude of other Packers and the team did not win.

All of this leads me to ask: "Just how good are Johnny Unitas and Bart Starr?" Don't get me wrong, I know that both Unitas and Starr are great, and I use the term "great" advisably. But would they have been winners with the Washington Redskins? Sonny Jurgensen, who has been quarterbacking the Redskins for five seasons, has been unable to win a championship for them. As far as I'm concerned, though, Jurgensen is the finest quarterback in the game. He is the only passer I truly stand in awe of. Sonny is an artist, a passer with a beautiful release, and a man who can do everything when it comes to throwing a football. It is his ill fortune to have been associated with players who do not measure up to his own high caliber. Because of this, he has been labeled as the type who can't win a championship. Had he been with the Colts or the Packers during the past decade Jurgensen would be regarded as the premier quarterback in football. I say this not to take anything away from Unitas or Starr but only to add a tribute long overdue to Sonny. What it all comes down to is that a great team makes a great quarterback.

Sammy Baugh says that the ideal quarterback would be one who could pass like Joe Namath and scramble like me. He says that if I could pass a little better I could be the best quarterback ever. How high I will rank when my career is over is impossible for anyone to know. I think that Baugh would be surprised to know how high I rank right now, for I know that I was pleasantly surprised. I'm not much for statistics, but my lawyer is and he came up with some interesting ones. He was trying to prove that all the emphasis on my being a scrambler has detracted from my ability as a passer. What he found out was that I have averaged more touchdown passes per season than any other quarterback in NFL history: 20.4 over an eight-year period. No. 2 on the all-time list is Unitas, who has averaged 19.5 scoring passes for 13 seasons. My lawyer also found that I rank fourth — using the rating scale now used to consider all categories of passing — among all quarterbacks in the history of the NFL. Starr, Unitas, and Jurgensen are the only three ahead of me on that list.

What a quarterback needs even more than an impressive set of statistics is a championship. It is only when he has helped his team to win a title that he gains real recognition. I think that the Giants are nearing the day when they will once again win a championsip and when they do my statistics will come under close scrutiny. Then, and only then, will people appreciate what I mean when I say that I can do more than just scramble.

Since coming to New York, I have improved

considerably as a quarterback. I think that Allie Sherman is as fine a coach of quarterbacks as there is. He teaches technique as well as any man I've ever known. Van Brocklin was such a natural passer and things came so easily to him that, perhaps as a result, he never spent enough time analyzing his game to be able effectively to pass his knowledge on to me. Norm learned from two of the game's real geniuses — Sid Gillman and Clark Shaughnessy — and he taught me a lot of football. I'm grateful for everything he passed on to me, but I've learned an awful lot since coming to the Giants. Although I *am* a scrambler, the art of knowing how to set up in the pocket is vitally important to me. I never became adept at setting up while with the Vikings, but once Sherman got hold of me he worked with me very hard on this. As a result, I can now set up faster. This has helped both my passing game and my scrambling. Because I get set up more quickly, I can see things sooner and get my passes off with more certainty. And, if I see that there are no open receivers, I can break out of the pocket sooner and start scrambling.

Few quarterbacks have good working relations with their coaches and I think that this is sad. Both have to be able to operate together, must understand one another, and must be in agreement on how to manipulate the team's offense. Working with Sherman has been a joy. He doesn't give me unlimited freedom (which would be bad), but he does give me a chance to exert myself. Sherman sends in plays during a game, but with the understanding that I can substitute selections of my own, and I frequently do just that. When people ask me which plays Sherman sent in and which I chose, I tell them, "The ones that didn't work were Sherman's and the ones that did work were the ones I called." When you are able to poke that kind of fun at your coach and have him smile about it, then you know that you are working under ideal conditions.

Sherman has not only tolerated my humor and taught me a lot of football, he has also been willing to back me up when I call a play that backfires. This is *very* important to a quarterback. If he can call a play and know that he won't be second-guessed by his own coach, it takes off a lot of the pressure. Sherman appreciates how much preparation a quarterback puts into each game because the two of us work so closely for so many hours. Lots of times during the course of a season I'll drive over to his house and the two of us will spend hours plotting game strategy. So, when it comes to gametime, he knows that I am aware of all the plays and all the moves the defense is likely to make against them. And he knows that when I substitute one of my plays for one of his it's for a good reason.

Aside from my trips to Sherman's house and

perhaps a quiet night out for dinner with my wife and some close friends now and then, I am a hermit during the football season. My off-season home is in Atlanta. During the season I rent a house in Greenwich, Connecticut, about a 20-minute drive from Sherman's home in Scarsdale, New York. I'm pretty much pure football from the start of the season until the end of the last game. For the single players, though, living in New York presents some problems. It's easy to get caught up in the pace of the City. You run to catch a cab, you have people pulling and tugging at you and life can get hectic before you realize it.

New York is a marvelous place to play football, but there are problems in the City that sometimes make it difficult. Because New York is such a vibrant, bustling metropolis, it is hard to have the same intimacy among players that teams in smaller cities enjoy. It's not that the players in Green Bay, Wisconsin, run around any less or drink any less together than those in New York or any other city. But, in New York the team is scattered over a wider area. Some of our players live in New Jersey, some in Connecticut, some in upstate New York, some in Manhattan, others on Long Island, and still others commute from Philadelphia.

When I was with the Vikings, all the players lived within about 10 minutes of one another and, as a result, our families were able to get together frequently and we had closer relationships. It was easier there to have cohesiveness than it is in New York, or in Los Angeles, or in Chicago. This is a limitation, because cohesiveness is important to a team. Another thing that has hurt somewhat is that the current Giant team is one that has been going through a transition. There has been a large turnover of personnel, players retiring, and new ones coming in and trying to establish themselves. It is important to know a player off the field as well as on to fully understand him. This takes time.

When Vince Lombardi was coaching in Green Bay, he ascribed much of his success to the fact that his players had "a great love for one another." It may not be love in the way most people think of it; but it is really a matter of pride and of feeling for one another. This sort of togetherness is cemented by off-the-field relationships.

Because our players are so spread out during the season, it is impossible to spend much time together. Therefore, we try to encourage players to get together as much as they can during preseason training. For instance, each Wednesday we have a cookout, where everyone can forget about football and game plans and have a night of relaxation together. I feel very close to Sherman, not only because I know how much he has helped me personally, but I know how hard he has tried to mold us into a team, into the sort of cohesive unit in which players have an empathy for one another. It isn't an easy job.

My first preseason practice with the Giants in that late summer of 1967 didn't exactly exhilarate me. After I had taken my first look at my new teammates, I found it hard to believe that this was a National Football League team. I had never seen worse playing personnel on any team, anywhere. We had much better players on the Vikings during our first season in the league. I thought that perhaps my first impressions of the Giants might have been incorrect, so I tried to be more observant in looking for positive points. It was no use. When I got back to my room at night I had an overwhelming desire to sit down and cry. "What in the world have I gotten myself into?" I asked myself over and over.

Well, for one thing, I had become a part of a team that in the previous season had compiled the worst record in the NFL: One win, one tie, and 12 losses. In 1966 the Giants had not only finished last, they had done so in convincing fashion. It was a team that was weak in almost every area. The Giants had finished next-to-last in kickoff returns, rushing defense, and punting, and third from the bottom in interceptions made and in pass defense. Only three teams had been worse in rushing than the Giants, and the top-ranked receiver on the club had placed 15th. That receiver, though, was Homer Jones, who had caught 48 passes and, more significantly, had been first in average yards gained per catch — 21.8. Anybody who could pick up yardage at that clip had to be something special and I anxiously looked forward to teaming up with Homer on pass plays. That ray of hope, however, was dimmed by the realization that the rest of the team was still short on talent. It was a team that, in the process of being outscored 501-263, had lost by such scores as 52-7 to Dallas, 55-14 to Los Angeles, and 72-41 to Washington.

Still, I like to be optimistic. I like to feel that every game I play is going to be a victory for my team. During those summer workouts, though, I had to look hard for signs of encouragement. We knew that our defense especially was in bad shape for 1967. And when our offensive units had a hard time scoring against our own defense during intra-squad games it began to look as though there was going to be a long, painful season ahead of us.

Then came our first regular-season game. It took place on a warm afternoon in St. Louis. The first time we had the ball we marched 76 yards to a touchdown, Bill Triplett carrying the ball the final four yards. Homer Jones was superb that day and my first touchdown pass for the Giants in league play was a 70-yarder that he latched on to. He wound up with five catches for the game, scored a second time, and we won 37-20. We were further encouraged when we built a 10-0 lead against Dallas in our next game. Although we lost that one 38-21, we knew that we were no longer a team that was going to lose a dozen games.

Two of our most significant games were in October, first against the Steelers and then against the Browns. In the Steeler game I suffered one of the few injuries of my career. Shortly before halftime I got clobbered on one of my scrambles and the pain in my back was so severe that I thought I was going to pass out in the locker room. I was given a shot and when the team went back on the field for the second half the best I could do was to walk behind my teammates as they sped off ahead of me. I told Allie I was going to play, but at the end of the third period it seemed futile. We trailed 24-14 and I wasn't much help. In the fourth quarter we weren't doing much better. Then, with four minutes left in the game, I ran seven yards for a touchdown. Two minutes later we recovered a fumble on our own 41. Before I went out on the field I huddled with Sherman. "What do you think?" I asked.

"The fleaflicker," he said.

"You've got to be kidding."

He wasn't kidding. I told our players we were going to use The Well Special — as our fleaflicker had been named in honor of Owner Wellington Mara. It's the kind of play that can send shivers through you just thinking about it and I'm sure that some of my teammates couldn't believe what I was saying. We may all have lacked confidence in the play, but the way we executed it was a delight to behold. I took the snap from center and handed off to halfback Ernie Koy, who then handed off to Homer Jones. This is exactly the way our end-around play to Jones began and we knew that the Steelers were familiar with that play. What they weren't familiar with, though, was the wrinkle that came next. As the Steelers prepared to defend against a run by Jones, he flipped the ball back to me. I looked downfield and what to my wondering eyes should appear but Joe Morrison all alone some 40 yards away. I threw the ball, Joe caught it, ran the remaining yards to the end zone, and we won 27-24. We have tried that same play twice since then and it hasn't come close to working. It did that day, though, and it was the single most spectacular play I have been involved in since joining the Giants.

Winning that game had a particular significance for me. It was the first time I had ever had to play despite a painful injury and it was comforting to know that I could do a respectable job. I'm sure that every player in our league has thought about the physical brutality of our game and I think we all feel a sense of pride in being able to overcome injury. It is the sort of thing that none of us looks forward to, but once we have passed

152

through these deep waters and proved to ourselves that we can endure, it is a rewarding experience.

Our finest victory of the 1967 season came against the Browns two weeks later. The Browns, who went on to finish first in the newly established Century Division, had given up only 85 points in their previous six games and when they went ahead of us 10-0 it seemed that we were out of contention. But our defense came through with some big plays, recovering three Cleveland fumbles, intercepting a pass, and stopping the Browns when it counted most. Our offense also performed, scoring 38 points against the formidable Cleveland defense in the final three periods, and we won 38-34.

When the season was all over, we were able to look back on a 7-7 record, a second-place finish in the Century, and an offense that had been outscored by only two other teams in the entire league.

We got off to a fast start in 1968, winning our first four games. It was the best beginning of a season by a Giant team in 27 years. One of the most meaningful passes I ever threw came against Washington in our third game of the season. Homer Jones had caught three passes in our first game and none in our second, a game in which the Eagles had double- and triple-teamed him all day. He had been working extra hard both in games and in practice sessions but he had yet to achieve what he wanted and needed most, namely, to catch a touchdown pass.

Well, the Redskins got into a blitz situation in the second quarter and I called an audible, hoping that I would find Homer in the open. I did. He caught my pass, turned on the afterburners, and scored on an 82-yard play. I knew how much that touchdown meant to him and I was so happy for him that I ran almost the length of the field to congratulate him. When I finally got to him on the sideline, I wrapped my arms around him and tried to lift him up. Unable to budge him, I contented myself with giving him a hug that I could only hope would convey my happiness.

After winning four straight, we were upset by Atlanta 24-21. It was one of the bitterest losses of my life. The game had meant a lot to me, for I was playing in Atlanta in front of people I had grown up with. And I was playing against Norm Van Brocklin for the first time. He had taken over as coach of the Falcons the week before. I'll admit that I wanted to beat Van Brocklin, but this is not really an admission. Every player wants to beat his former coach or his former teammates more than he wants to beat people he hardly knows. Some of the best friends I have ever had are still with the Vikings and because they are I want to be at my best when I play them. Against the Falcons that day I had my chance to get the victory I wanted so badly and which we needed to stay in a first-place tie with Dallas. We trailed by three points late in the game and had moved from our own 10-yard line down to the Falcon 18. With 90 seconds to go, I threw a pass that was intercepted and that was the end of our winning streak.

In November we rallied to upset Dallas 26-21. That left us just one game behind the Cowboys in the Capitol Division (the NFL had undergone another realignment), but we were unable to improve our second-place ranking as we once again closed out the season with a 7-7 record.

I have learned a lot during my two years with the Giants. One of the major changes in my philosophy as a quarterback is that I no longer believe there is any such thing as a primary receiver. I now feel that every eligible receiver is a so-called primary receiver. The only thing that determines my No. 1 receiver is the reaction of the defense. If they give me a man-to-man coverage on a certain pattern, then my flanker may be my receiver. If they give me a strong-side zone on the same pattern, it may be that I should throw to my tight end. I believe that there is always someone open on a pass pattern if the quarterback can read the defense properly. Unhappily, quarterbacks are imperfect people, and we don't always find that open man.

Some people ask me why I don't just throw

the bomb to Homer Jones all day long. I don't because the game is changing and it isn't possible any more. The big bomb used to be thrown much more frequently in earlier years. Van Brocklin threw it all the time to Elroy Hirsch and others. Unitas used to pump and throw the long one to Lenny Moore and to Raymond Berry. You can't do that any longer, even though there are faster receivers than ever before, men who can go 9.2, 9.3, 9.4.

It's because pro teams are increasingly going to zone-type defenses: There are pure zones, strong-side zones, weak-side zones, and combination man-to-man zones. Very seldom do you have man-to-man situations as you did years ago. This is the way the defense has been trying to counter the speed of men such as Jones. I'd love to spend all day throwing to him — if it would lead to a win for the Giants. As it is, we have him going deep on almost all pass patterns. But, while we're doing this, we also have other men running other patterns. When I see that they haven't zoned to Homer's side — I can see this as soon as I get the snap — and that they are giving him just man-to-man coverage, that's when he's my man. Any time we can get Homer with just one man on him, we've got it made. But if they *have* zoned to his side of the field, it means that there must be single coverage on some other receiver and that's where I'll be looking to throw. I want to go to the place where I've got the best odds of completing a pass and avoiding an interception.

I said that I've learned a lot in the past two seasons, but I think I should also point out that football is a game in which you are constantly aware that you have only a limited amount of ability and that you have never learned enough. Whenever I start thinking that I do a good job of scrambling, I have only to remind myself of the day that Merlin Olsen of the Rams, who is 6′ 5″ and 275 pounds caught me *from behind*. Then, too, there was the day when my memory failed me during my first year with the Giants. I called a play in the huddle and told one of my teammates I wanted him to "George" block. That's a special kind of blocking between center and guard. My teammate said, "What?"

I snapped back, "I said we're running F-30 and I want you to George block."

Again he said, "What?"

This time I yelled at him, "George block it." Then, as we broke the huddle and headed for the line I realized that "George" block was the terminology we used when I was with the Vikings and that on the Giants the same blocking was called a "Blue" block. Football was a way of humbling all of us.

Our team has come a long way during the past two years, not so much because I have been a part of it as because of the fine coaching of Allie Sherman and the intelligent manner in which the team has drafted and traded. Our defense, once a shambles, has tightened up considerably. No longer do I have to look at my teammates and shake my head. Ours is a solid club, one that has been in the running for a divisional title until well past midseason during the past two years. It won't be long before that title — and perhaps much more — will be ours.

Above all, I am constantly stimulated by the realization that football can excite me as much as it does. I've played hundreds of games — from the sandlots, through high school and college, and now with the pros. Still, there is always a thrill in completing a pass, or scoring a touchdown, or winning a ball game. As long as those thrills are there I hope to keep on passing and, when I have to, scrambling.